BOOT SALE HARVEST

Adrian May

DUNLIN PRESS

BOOT SALE HARVEST

Published by Dunlin Press in 2023

Dunlin Press
Wivenhoe, Essex
dunlinpress.com | @dunlinpress

The right of the Adrian May to be identified as the author of this work
has been asserted in accordance with Section 77 of the Copyright,
Designs and Patents Act 1988.

A CIP record of this book is available from the British Library.

ISBN: 978-1-7394038-0-5

Set in Highgate and Adobe Garamond Pro.
Book illustration and design by Ella Johnston. Photography by MW Bewick.

BOOT SALE HARVEST

A psycho-antiquarian journal of recent
literary and cultural excavation

FOREWORD

by Ken Worpole

If we ever thought a book was needed on car boot sales then poet, folklorist, literary academic, hobbyist, musician and collector of trifles, Adrian May, was clearly the writer to do it. And now he has, quite wonderfully. Exploring the lost and found of everyday life in early 21st century Britain, he has alchemised base lead into anthropological gold. As May writes early on, 'everything is interesting'. This is his home counties' version of Marx's famous dictum (based on the Roman philosopher's *humani nihil a me alienum puto*): nothing human is alien to me. Stuff may be simply stuff to some people but it is made up of memories, affections, interests, transitional objects, souvenirs, relics and icons – of lives led, lost or relocated to pastures new.

The author sets out his stall at a respectful distance from the academy, where material culture and 'rubbish theory' are now serious areas of study, though he is too lively a thinker and writer not to have also learned from the insights of anthropology and semiotics. In the serendipitous inventories of purchases which introduce each chapter, May magics up strange, timeless worlds where stop watches rub shoulders with children's poetry, second-hand radios, OS maps, music hall records, Royal Doulton soup bowls, and bargain-price tins of beans. A whole set of novels could be conjured out of the inventories in the book, so rich is this harvest. May further reclaims a 20th century folkloric tradition of his own, crossing the divides between comic song, folk song, ancient myths and legends, fairy tales, rock and roll, and the essays of now overlooked authors such as Richard Church and Richard Hughes, or more recent esoteric writers such as Dawn Ades or Dion Fortune. We also learn that he seems to survive on a diet of new potatoes and fresh strawberries.

Anthropologist Mary Douglas once famously wrote that "dirt is matter out of place", and though the concept was already familiar – if less pithily expressed – Douglas gave it lasting significance. Thus, she argued, a newspaper on a breakfast table is a high cultural object but when using to wrap a portion of chips, or laid on the floor to stand a pair of muddy boots on, it loses status instantly. The objects at car boot sales are clearly in an ambiguous position: out of place but still in transition, and currently of no fixed abode. Furthermore, they now mix promiscuously with other objects of equally indefinite status, no longer part of an established 'order of things'. And finally, they are outdoors, where most of them don't belong, but which, paradoxically, the Covid pandemic legitimised as a new safe space, when most other public meeting places were fenced off by a cordon sanitaire. Boot sales have popular antecedents, being new versions of the traditional street market, flea market or 'waste', the last being an even poorer version of the same thing, historically held on bomb-sites or derelict slum land.

There are in *Boot Sale Harvest* similar elements of the delight which millions found in the critically acclaimed television series, *Detectorists*. A large part of May's own treasure trove trawls up related local searches and gazetteers – of local history, parish churches, guides to flora and fauna, archaeology and myths – all of which point to an abiding interest that many have with the minutiae of local life stretching back to the mythical past. Like metal detecting, this passion for knowing who came before us and how they made sense of the local inhabited landscape - the homes they lived in, the way they dressed, the beliefs they held, religious or mystical, the troubles they had, and the catastrophes visited upon them – is largely beneath the radar of an increasingly globalised media culture, but it is still felt by many to have a continuing bearing on the way we live now. The investment people still have in the idea of 'the local' often finds its own rewards close to hand.

It appears that boot sales have expanded the market in second-hand goods to include a multitude of new buyers and sellers, creating another niche in the recycling and repair economy. These range from occasional sellers who may be moving house or down-sizing, to semi-professional dealers. In addition, there are the house clearance specialists who, according to May, usually occupy their own patch. A degree of unsentimentality is required when it comes to certain items, particularly the many anonymous family photo albums now common on some stalls. This have now been cut adrift from their original owners, leaving the people and scenes portrayed cruelly nameless and homeless. I am told that there are now people who voluntarily or professionally offer to re-trace the original owners of unidentified albums that have ended up on second-hand stalls, and if that is true this is an interesting new development in the ongoing renewal of family history. The aura of melancholy that surrounds these and other personal items recalls Hemingway's famous suggestion, when offered a bet to write the shortest story ever: "For sale: baby shoes, never worn."

One question goes unanswered in the book. Where does the author find room for this never-ending list of acquisitions?* All we know is that he has a deep stairwell in his flat, room enough for a long ladder and space for hanging new pictures. But where does he put the rest of the stuff – all the second-hand books, notebooks, guitars, ukuleles, crockery, and numerous accoutrements of the never- ending folk-music revival in which he has always played his part? Readers of *Boot Sale Harvest* will wish him well in 'curating' his many new acquisitions, and thank him for the pleasure of reading this quirky, affectionate account of one of British culture's more recent outdoor ritual gatherings, which as the author confirms, is less about commerce and more about community. What goes around comes around.

Ken Worpole is a writer and social historian whose most recent book is *No Matter How Many Skies Have Fallen: Back to the Land in Wartime Britain* (2021).

---

*I pass much on, as in the chapter on 'Gifts'. Ken himself says, "It's all about circulation, the gift is only meaningful if it is not kept but passed on." See, for example, one of our mutual favourite books, *The Gift* by Lewis Hyde. Though I do also have lots of books… A.M.

In memory of 'Ukulele' Dave Sibley

Week 1: WORLD MYTH

WEDNESDAY 14TH APRIL 2021. MARKS TEY.

Myths and Legends. Roger Lancelyn Green, Puffin
(4 volumes, boxed). 50p.

Parker black ink cartridges. £1.

New winter hat with earflaps. £5

2 Wedgwood soup bowls. £2.

Large Staffordshire soup bowl. £1.

Pub. ed. Angus McGill. 50p.

Walking stick. £1.

The Lawrence Wright's 20 Song and Dance Album
(1929). £1.

Ian Campbell Folk Group Songbook (1965). £1.

FRIDAY 16TH APRIL 2021. HORSLEY CROSS.

Green exercise book; new. 50p.

The Prelude. William Wordsworth
(Penguin, parallel text). 50p.

24 bags of peanuts on card. £4.

Hand sanitizer. £1.

The first boot sale of my year was a good one, but it was hard to get a stallholder's attention, as they were all talking to each other in the excitement of the new season. In the past year, boot sales had become one of the few safe or safe-ish public places where you could mingle with the world. I was happy to be back wandering in the spring, with hopes of a good year among them, aware of how central boot sales had become to my life and thought.

Boot sales had long been for me a kind of contemporary cultural antiquarianism. I was an antiquarian who studied recently discarded objects and texts for clues to his own place and time, his own recent history. Or maybe just an old booter, or rummager or rootler. Yes, I could be an eccentric but that's normal in England.

This isn't a story about money, or about 'antiques and collectables', though bargains are to be had. It's not 'upcycling', more a kind of restoration of significance. "The task of the hero," said Jessie Weston in *From Ritual to Romance* (1920) "is that of restoration". It is more to do with creative poverty. I am more a scavenger and ponderer of the recently discarded world, discovering invaluable artefacts amid the ruins like a scavenger for overlooked truth. And I miss Theo, a friend's small black dog, as he had the same aim of finding dropped but still fragrant trifles. For him, a half-discarded hot-dog, for me an old pamphlet of local history, for example. He loved going to boot sales, and so do I.

Writing now at the end of the season, on a rainy day in October, I feel I might write mournful waltzes about the

year's sales, about the lost festive, cheerful world of stuff –
a world that values itself above the stuff, above any goods,
somehow. A jolly, sweet, small bargain is not merely material.
I can take you into this world of lost and found and guide
you through my own meandering pathos, where I find most
of life, so much of life and of myself.

There's always something new to see, something to learn,
something to teach you its lesson and sing you its old song.
This humblest of worlds is also an astonishing one and I
have a long history of delving deeply into it.

My first purchase on the first boot sale of the year, as you
can see above, was a slightly scuffed, well-read box of myths
and legends. Many years of jumbles, charity shops and boot
sales had brought me here, as well as many years of reading
and teaching the value, the incalculable value of myths as
artefacts from the past. Now my mind was taken straight
to that wealth in a magic box full of old tales which still
resonate with me. I knew of Lancelyn Green's collections but
had never owned any. This was partly because the 'myths for
children' subtext detracted from my own attitude of myth
as an active force in the world now. Student: "Everything is
myth then, Adrian." Me: "Too right, mate!"

I saw the attitude that myths and fairy stories were not for
adults as a kind of 'mythic hiding', where the real truths of
myth (and everything) were hiding in places of insignificance,
like boot sales or the kids' section of a bookshop. Myths
and truths disappear into triviality, into the overlooked. A

boxed set of books is lovely, like a metaphor of significance, of magic, that must be kept in a box. Specialness is given to what is in a box. Pandora's box was a clay vessel, but genies of hope and despair are in there. The set of myths and legends seem to have been given by a teacher to a favoured pupil in 1971. In 1971 I was being told by my first proper girlfriend and my best male friend of the significance of fairy tales and myths. I always hung out with those more intelligent than me. I never forgot their lesson and even made a career and some books of my own out of it.

It would have been the following year, 1972, that another inspiring friend first took me to a jumble sale. Fiona was a textile designer and always on the lookout for the history of design, for unusual fabrics and for the inspiring ideas to be got from public art. She went to look for old dresses, pieces of fabric, Victorian patterns, textures and colours. I still have a painting she made of Neptune, copied from an old fairground item she noticed in a warehouse in London. She was passing and went into ask if she could draw some of the items stored. She always had her Rotring pen and a black sketchbook with her. I was inspired by her at the jumble in Muswell Hill, London, where we shared a flat. I bought lovely 1930s men's fine Viyella scarves, one green with white polka dots. These I had to wash with disinfectant, as I realised men rarely washed outer clothing in the 30s and 40s. I bought old football and rugby shirts to wear as tops, before the ubiquity of T-shirts and polo shirts in the shops. Probably a book or two. Most things were 10p and we both came away happy, sharing our excitement at both bargains and our eye for lovely, discarded items. She created in me a whole area of culture that was to become a constant in my life, as well as, eventually, a whole world for me after everything seemed to be ending.

Endings come all at once and multiply, like a mythic decline. In *Myths of the Norsemen*, Lancelyn Green tells of "when the whole world would perish on a day – the day of Ragnarok, the Twilight of the Gods – the Day of the Last Great Battle" and "the Doom, which was to overtake them". I had first looked at this one of the four volumes because of my interest in Iduna (or Idun) and the Apples of Youth. Now my thoughts go to the endings, as that seems the mythic world we found ourselves in during the pandemic dooms of our time. My 50p myth boxed set reminds me of everything.

Some of the endings were my own. In December 2019, I had all but retired from my job as a university teacher of myth and creativity at Essex University, just before my 70th birthday. My band Face Furniture and the Extensions played a gig on my birthday in January 2020, which felt like a last gig anyway. I gave a talk about apples of youth at the Essex Book Festival, which now seems an irony. Then the world closed in the first lockdown. On the day after my birthday, also, my ex partner had written me a letter telling me she did not love me, effectively coming back to tell me she'd gone. More endings. They seem to multiply in my mind. I had planned to swan in for coffee with my two retained PhD students and other pals on campus, and to chat with my bookselling pal about latest finds, but all that ended before it began.

The only thing starting was my book about tradition. I took to the boot sales, nervously, but began to find everything there. I even wrote about boot sales a bit in *Tradition in Creative Writing* – originally titled *Roots Writer: How to be Traditional*. The idea for writing about boot sales gained ground.

After my introduction to the joys of jumble by my artist friend, I moved out of London and became a slightly eccentric dresser, in my stylish scarves and green duffle coat. This had been bought for me by Fiona and her boyfriend Mike, as they knew I liked green things. It was a good brand and it lasted for years. Some girls I later got to know actually used to call me 'Green Duffle Coat' before we ever spoke. The other notable buy was a bicycle, in working order, for £5. All these things, including moving out of London, turned me into someone dreaming their way into having a culture of my own. I looked back, you could say, but to me it was more looking sideways, or differently, as well as looking different.

Mainly it was fun. I found my first bone china tea-plate to use after cycling to Bocking village hall. I began to find books of all kinds. Later in the 1970s, charity shops began to appear. These were great sources of collarless shirts, just before they became trendy, as well as good tweed jackets. I bought real dungarees, while others bought denim ones at

10 times the price. Books were a constant.

In the 1980s I remember boot sales beginning. By then I had started buying records, mainly in charity shops. Old music-hall artists, a compilation of Noel Gay hits, Paddy Roberts' comic songs and 78s of anything comic, such as 'You Can't Do That There Here' educated me. My musical career began with me tracing the roots of English songwriting, particularly comic songwriting, through the previous generations' work and listening. I often felt alone in my interest, but my swimming against the tide was both bracing and a way to self-locate.

By the time I got to my regular local boot sales, much of my own sense of self came with the help of these discoveries. I was used to keeping quiet about it, though. An old girlfriend pointed out that even when I earned a reasonably good salary and didn't need to buy cheap or secondhand, I still acted poor. New things have built-in disappointment, as well as often built-in obsolescence. The shod of the new! Elvis hated antiques, having been brought up poor, among old stuff. I don't blame him for having everything synthetic in Graceland. We have a similar feel for the rush of newness, which is an illusion of course. I think my Bohemian upbringing, gentle if not genteel, amid old books, making do, and a farmer's distrust of innovation formed me. My dad had a writer's outlook, where good work was the thing. The latest thing is the thing that doesn't work yet, to paraphrase Douglas Adams.

One current example: I recently played an old tune called

'Epping Forest' at a concert. This I had found on 78 at a jumble sale in Theydon Bois. Me and my partner Angela often went there in the mid 1970s. Rich areas are good for jumble and this one would yield designer-like clothes for her as well as priceless 78s for me. This one cost little and was by the BBC Wireless Military Band, arranged and conducted by the great folk collector Cecil Sharp. I still have it.

So the old boot sale had become a key to me. In my university job, I knew no-one who shared this interest. It seems now that only women artists (and a few male poets) get it, and I've had some fun adventures of finding with some of them, now and again. I accept my solitary wayfarer's journey to these islands of off-grid recycling, these secretly festive exchanges of old and new selves. These were spaces I could dream in, feel part of the crowd yet also apart from everything, and connect to the soul of the world and its myth.

Before I became a university teacher, I had been, for a few years, a paid manager of a charity bookshop. This was a dream job for me and I loved it. Many of my volunteer staff loved books and old things like I did. I met some book experts, runners and dealers. We found priceless first editions and sold them at auction for the hospice. We held silent auctions of rare local books and sold rare records after playing them on our donated high-end hi-fi system. This also played 78s. I have a fond memory of my expert volunteers and me listening to the Winfield label's cover of Bill Haley's 'Don't

Knock the Rock', as sold in Woolworths in the 1950s. We were knocked out by the brilliance of it, when we'd assumed it would be no good. Those jazzer session guys could play. I still went to boot sales and, where books were concerned, gained a bit more knowledge of potential value.

Boot sales are enough out of the world to have their own distinct feel, always changing, always about recovery, rediscovery and for me, self-discovery. They have humility built in but the riches are endless and ordinary. The blind followers of the new will accuse you of nostalgia, which only means a yearning for home. By and large, it isn't a sentimental world but is open-minded enough to give acknowledgement to the past in the present. The modern world is there too, in its discarded way, in its dealers on the make.

The other thing people accuse you of is being a hoarder. Many have bare homes. There is not much useful or beautiful in their idealistic lives, except their aspirations and vacant spaces. People assume you have houses full of useless things. I do have lots of books and musical instruments, not all bought secondhand either, but everything is interesting. Sometimes I say "I'm not a hoarder, but I'm on the border", but I'm a modest, careful buyer, enjoying the strange and the old, useful items. A visitor recently admired how my place reflects my interests; a female friend compared it to a preserved artist's studio. New things are sold at boot sales too and the serendipity sometimes seems to verge into magic alignment, when you tune in and find the right book for your latest interest. It is more about love than stuff, a way of being in relation to the world, the bigger myth.

I have often thought, over the years, of writing about boot sales, jumbles and charity shops, but found it hard to find a way in that didn't sound corny or trite. I took my own advice and found something specific, finally. At Marks Tey a few years back, in May, I had gone with a female work friend, a note-taker rather than an academic, and we strolled down by the hedge towards the stalls from the car parking area. I realised that the bird I could hear singing was a nightingale. My song 'Bootsale Nightingale' seemed to emerge naturally from this and I managed to say some of the things I wanted to about the whole experience. Later, a friend remarked that I was the only songwriter she knew who could get the word 'inexorable' into a song and get away with it. Usefully, it is a song about love.

BOOT-SALE NIGHTINGALE

We roamed, not knowing what we might find
A change of scene or a change of mind
Then sang that bird you hear little of
His sharp and tremulous song of love
    He only sings for a mate, I said
    As lovely springtime filled my head
    It felt so poignant, it felt so true
    And free to share it all with you

Arm in arm at the old boot-sale
We heard the song of the nightingale

We just stood there, caught up at last
No fear of future, no pain of past
Once you've heard it you always know
There's so much still that we might let go
  Every year the boot-sale's here
  Discarded riches of life appear
  A book for you, an old thing for me
  But his lovely singing was all for free
Arm in arm at the old boot-sale
We heard the song of the nightingale

The moment passed, but the air seemed rare
So normal having a love to share
The old and easy free for all
So cheap, so valued, so huge, so small
  Nature's inexorable metaphor
  Brings yearning to our open door
  So for love we must sing always
  And any season is spring these days
Arm in arm at the old boot-sale
We heard the song of the nightingale

Now that everything was ending, I felt the overwhelming
need for my simple alternative outside, public world. Many
people, me included, stopped tuning in to the news. "We

are informed about everything. We know nothing." This is from Saul Bellow's book *To Jerusalem and Back* (1976; p34). Guess where I bought it (see Week 15)? Boot sales were places that retained their sanity, their down-to-earth quality, their jaunty cocked-hat of cast-off glory, and a constant in a changing world. The boot sale had hope – and little bargains to cheer the heart.

I was planning a new book about the lost world of what is public, and boot sales were to be a chapter. When I told a friend about this, he thought boot sales were to be the theme of a whole book. When this happened more than once, my mind built on these mistakes, treating them as my hidden intention. But, a whole book about boot sales? Really? At first the idea seemed absurd.

I'm writing from notes written in the green notebook, bought above for 50p. Some of my original notes and all my boot sale logs are in a hardbacked old blue notebook, bought for £1 a few years' back, I think at Marks Tey. It has lovely thick paper and feels good to write in. I was actually using a new uni-ball Gel Impact 1mm pen, but I could have easily used my £2 Parker Flame, bought a few years ago in the Weeley boot sale, using an ink cartridge, as bought above. I correct a print-out on a lovely East-Light ply clipboard, made in England, £1.

The only book I've seen on boot sales, is one about finding valuable goods, and online there is a very dull economic paper about the recycling aspect. Is this one a psychogeography? Maybe more a psycho-cultural contemporary antiquarianism, or just the tales of an old rubbish picker, bigging himself up. The best books that might be a bit like this are *Cadillac Jack* (1982) by Larry McMurtry and *My Old Man's a Dustman* (1956) by Wolf Mankowitz. The former about an antique dealer and the later about a totter, which means someone who scavenges scrap heaps.

In the 1980s I used to write, in pencil, the place, date and price in the books I bought. McMurtry's book I found new in a shop that used to have a spinner of US paperbacks, mostly of the pulp variety. It wasn't published in the UK properly until later. My Pocket edition is 1988, bought by me in '89 for 99p. I must have read Mankowitz's book from a library, but I do have *The Penguin Wolf Mankowitz* (1967), bought in Epping Flea Market in 1985 for 40p. Both this and *Cadillac Jack* have interesting front matter. "I am a forty-two year old Russian-Jewish-English-Scorpio professional freelance writer. Need I say more?" says Mankowitz, while McMurtry dedicates his book to "Diane Keaton, Queen of the Swap-Meets". Both give the right flavour of wit and engagement and I feel both are with me here as I write.

The echo of English-flavoured rock, there in Mankowitz who wrote the film (and book) *Expresso Bongo* (1959), is also in his *My Old Man's a Dustman*. This title, from a kids' chant, was turned into a hit by Lonnie Donegan (see Week 12). Written in a folklorist way by himself and his manager with Leslie Bricusse, who also wrote lots of stuff with Tony Newley. The Ian Campbell book has English rock connections too, or rather English reggae, his sons later forming UB40. The book features an item called 'A Garland of Children's Street Songs', reminding me again of Donegan's and Mankowitz's title.

Epping Flea Market, in those days on Saturdays, was a favourite haunt and source of the Penguin Mankowitz. In the antique centre attached I bought my favourite stage-use ukulele for £8, now worth hundreds; a mahogany Aloha Royal, as played by Elvis on the poster of *Blue Hawaii*. With nice synchronicity, among the songs in *The Lawrence Wright 20th Song and Dance Album*, are the words and music of Leslie Sarony's 'Jollity Farm'. This would have been among the first songs I played on the uke at the time of buying it.

I have found life back in the old boot sale. I have found friends, gifts aplenty, food, dishes to eat food from, music, transport, clothes, tools, DIY projects, cases, bags, boxes, furniture, secrets, inspiration, libraries, history, locality, exotic curios, nightingales, songs, my ancestors, new hats, stationery, office equipment, art, laughs, philosophy, banality – even bargains worth hundreds for a few pounds or pence. A boot sale is a big poem. These are among the tales I'll be telling. The love and the fun and the finding, the innocence of the wanderer, the suspension from the onrush towards the latest crash, the universality of the ordinary, the overlooked, the sweet discarded worlds on their islands of grass. Maybe I should say 'Boot Fair', as my friend Jo does. It is a passing show that holds all hope, a respite from the curse of the grim, normal world of today's conventions. I also found the big world myth, even in this first week.

Come with me and we'll see what we can find. Here is the irredeemably human. Is the day fair? It's not far. Let us go.

Flowers of St. Francis

THOUGHTS FROM THE ANCIENTS

Christina Rossetti

MATTHEW ARNOLD

LAST POEMS

Goethe's
"Faust"
and
Minor
Poems

The
Canterbury
Poets

Cloth
1/3 net

Walter Sco

Week 2: STOP-WATCH

WEDNESDAY 21ST APRIL 2021. MARKS TEY.

Stop-watch. £25.

English Inns (Britain in Pictures). Free with above.

Ghost Road. Pat Barker. 50p.

Zuleika Dobson. Max Beerbohm. (Old Penguin, 50p).

The Hidden River. Storm Jameson. (as above).

Making Cocoa for Kingsley Amis. Wendy Cope. 50p.

The Ballad of the White Horse. G.K. Chesterton. £1.

Gilbert Keith Chesterton. Maisie Ward. £1.

Elements of Fly Fishing for Trout and Greyling. 50p.

PVA glue. £1.

Floella lavender disinfectant. £1.

FRIDAY 23RD APRIL (ST GEORGE'S DAY). HORSLEY CROSS.

Nothing.

I don't get up that early. I don't rush. I walk slow. I'm not keen; I'm not at work. You will find your own way if you take it. People have different rhythms. It should be fun.

What do you need? Shoes that can bear being dusty and a bit of wear. A fairly capacious bag with a spare extra bag in it, some cash with some small change including plenty of 50p and £1 coins. Getting in is usually 50p or £1. A few layers that can come off, if needed. Some sunblock. That's about it really. Some take smartphones, cameras, notebooks, magnifying loops, lists of wants or gaps in collections. Water, snack bars, biscuits, glucose sweets if you need them. A hat is useful, or essential for me. I keep it light and easy as I can. I also have a green Fiat Qubo, which is easy to spot in the car-park (it is common to get lost trying to find your car in a big field) but that's not essential. All you need's some spare change and some dusty shoes / Then you'll get the boot sale blues. You're welcome.

I usually get there between eight and nine. Keen dealers, the sellers and those trying to make a living get there early, or stupid-o-clock. We're doing a more relaxed thing here, aiming to sink in and a become open to the whole carnival of ordinary unwanted stuff that is to be our little world. Follow the signs, park where you're told. Wander gently with your eyes open. No obligations – a sense of wonder and of humanity are your most useful assets.

Stroll down the lines at will but with an eye to where you've been and not been. At a big boot sale like Marks Tey there's loads to see. I usually head for where I know the house clearance people have big stalls. There you get the fresh, unusual stuff and sometime loads of books, sometimes none.

Unusually for me, this week I went with an agenda. I wanted a stop-watch. You'll have guessed by now that I'm not one for timing my early morning sprint. I write songs and I need to time them sometimes, as part of the composing process. Concision is part of the art. When I started as a singer-songwriter (snigger snog-writer, as my mocker pals say), I used to time my stuff not to be longer than 3 mins 30 secs in length. Most that went over were cut. I'd had a digital stop-watch, designed I guess for sports persons, but they break down and run out of battery, besides being ugly as hell. I had decided to buy an old fashioned stop-watch, one that looks like a proper pocket watch. The first stall I stopped at had some, to my delight.

Sometimes, when your mind is calm, things find you. The mature chap selling had some old books, which I looked at first. Ah, a book on pubs. I had found one last week (see Week 1). This was in the Britain in Pictures series. They used to be collectable, but the kind of old guys that collected them are gone now. They used to be a fiver or upwards for rare ones, like the one written by George Orwell. The second-hand price for a standard one now is about £2. The chap wanted £4 for this one, so I put it down and put him down a bit in my mind as being old-school, though that's no bad thing really, pot-to-kettle wise. I moved to the main part of his stall from the book box on the ground. Ah, watches! I asked if he had any stop-watches. He suddenly seemed keen and got two out. I told him I didn't like the modern ones and I felt I didn't have to explain about the manky plastic monstrosities sold in sports shops. I immediately chose the plainer one. £25 was cheaper than most on eBay, where good ones go for £50 and upwards. He patiently explained its obvious workings, when asked. I agreed to the price, then, on a whim, I asked if he'd throw in the pub book. With our recent found friendliness, he agreed. I guess he didn't sell many watches these days. People only wear expensive ones to show off; they use their phones for the time. The stop-watch has a £38 sticker on the back. Stylish old-style quality comes cheap.

My stop-watch works great, is Swiss-made with seven jewels, from a London retailer. I made a shed-craft stand for it, using a small block of off-cut deal from some shelving and a leaning back lid from a peanut butter jar, painted silver and lined with some green felt. Now I can see it as I time a new song. Have you any idea of how happy this is? Hope so.

Now I'm writing about boot sales, what I hadn't previously noticed in the everyday goings and buyings suddenly reveals itself as being full of significance. It occurs to me now, as I see fruits on the hedgerows, that it is harvest-time and I'm reaping my harvest-home. Little piles of books remain around my place, like wheat in stooks, waiting to be threshed for good grain.

The new winter hat bought in Week 1 has been tried

by now, half way through October. It is serious, German camouflage green, cosy as hell and the Velcro chin-strap is loath to come off. My cycling in the first chills of winter was warmed by hopeful buying from Week 1. There's a half-year rhythm here, which I feel I can move in.

Of our time but happy, the stallholder and I said thanks and I moved on. G.K. Chesterton had also been on my mind and I had decided that his epic ballad was something I needed a copy of, after reading it online. I had a few of his books from over the years. *Poems* bought in the 1980s, containing 'The Secret People' and 'The Rolling English Road' and various collections of essays. He wrote about England and so did I. He was seen as out-of-date and so was I. A theme of time emerges. Most of this stuff is out of print.

Another book I had was a paperback of *Orthodoxy*, which is the best argument for religion I have ever encountered. I had quoted him at length in my book on tradition (*Tradition in Creative Writing*, 2021). I liked chalk figures, especially in Eric Ravilious's paintings of them, as well as those I encountered in the landscape. It was ordinarily amazing that the next timed-out but timely stall I stopped at had a lovely heavy hardback with dust jacket of the epic ballad for £1. Thick paper, illustrations, big black print, substantial and just what I was looking for. This gets better. A few stalls along, from some antique dealer clearance chaps I often buy from (see Week 3), I found a Chesterton biography of similar condition and price. It was a big, detailed book, with an entry or two on *The Ballad of the White Horse*. This was a very good week, or I was well-tuned into what I wanted, somehow.

There's no need to hurry to old-time stuff at a boot sale. Few are looking for it in the way we are. At Marks Tey there is usually a good posh-coffee stall and plenty of food and drinks on sale. We can stop if we want. Taking your time is essential, for me, or you miss so much. I don't normally spend a big sum first off or even find what I knew I wanted, so this day is a better day, a timely day. You need items you can jump off from. Never have things in your home you can't jump off from. That's a better, more timely rule.

The two substantial volumes associated with Chesterton are not first editions. *The Ballad* is the 10th, from 1928, though the first illustrated edition (Robert Austin). The biography is a second edition, second reprint. Both obviously sold loads. They are indicators of a time before modernistic pessimism became the dominant thing in literary culture. Chesterton is mostly remembered now as the originator of the Father Brown stories. He was, maybe like J.B. Priestley, one of those allegedly 'middlebrow' writers who were both highly intelligent and popular.

The Ballad is right up my street, with its positive Englishness and chalk figure at the centre. The artist Eric Ravilious had painted chalk figures and had lived in Essex. His wife Tirzah was, I think, buried at the lovely Copford church, which is the nearest one to the Marks Tey boot sale. I had, some years' back, visited the Wilmington Giant chalk figure in Sussex and been moved and fascinated by it. Some photocopies of Ravilious's figures are on the wall of my office. The illustrator of my copy does not give you a picture of the Vale of the White Horse, and I understand that this oldest and strangest of the chalk figures is not easy to view. It is a minimal, abstract figure, like a Picasso almost, in its outline depiction. Ravilious's painting of it shows it disappearing or appearing, at the top of a slope, partially hidden, as if it is flying away from the landscape, or part of the sky. I had planned to visit the area but was thwarted by bad health and did not go. Other endings, in the deaths of friends and family, had come. The chalk figures' endurance now seems of increasing significance.

The poem itself must be due for a comeback. I could see a serious animated film musical. The poem is lyrical, easy reading. The lines are flexible too, like old ballads, flexing between four and six lines. The whole thing flows and is full of resonant phrases, like "Too English to be true" and the folk-song sounding "I tell you naught for your comfort". It is a myth of English origin that could be used in a respectful acknowledgement of ourselves, to honour our brave Scottish, Welsh and Irish neighbours' senses of self with our own bit of positive, inclusive character. Chesterton's introduction has the pithy 'controversialist' attitude claimed on the back cover. His essays are funny and thought-provoking and very fair in their lack of easy prejudice. If you see any, grab them, as there'll be something to engage you. Also from the boot sale, a few years ago I read his autobiography, similarly entertaining.

He makes the point that the poem is about popular legend not history, and has a claim therefore on tradition, which is still alive, as traditions must be. He has the same attitude as recent folk singers and storytellers. as he is dealing with the connection of King Alfred with the Vale of the White Horse, the playing of the harp in the enemy's camp by Alfred and the tale of the cakes. "I only seek to write upon a hearsay, as the old balladists did." Could the whole thing be sung? Could it be a folk opera? I'm still enjoying reading it. Chesterton thought, reports his biographer Maisie Ward, that myth and tradition could deal with the "big things", where history and facts deal in details.

The poem had become folk-like in its popularity, as Ward's biography tells (p245): "During the first world war many soldiers had it with them in the trenches: 'I want to tell you,' the widow of a sailor wrote, 'that a copy of the *Ballad*... went down into the Humber with the R.38. My husband loved it as his own soul – never went anywhere without it.'" Ward tells how people quoted its forebodings of war on the eve of the second world war (p246).

Later in the summer, I carried out my plan to draw a Wilmington-style giant in outline on the large, high stairwell of my upstairs maisonette. This is the kind of place where people used to hang a large brass-rubbing in the 1970s, I'm told. I had to brace myself to climb a long ladder, sketch in chalk before painting my outline, dark green on the yellow walls. I'm pleased with the result of what I call the Hythe Giant, after the area of Colchester where I live. I might set some of the poem to music.

St George's day came on that Friday and I was off to Horsley Cross, a much smaller boot sale but, given where I had been in my chalk-figure head, an appropriate place to dream of visions of a left-wing England, where Chesterton was recognised. I drove past Old School Road in Elmstead, then towards Harwich past a multi-language sign for those coming from the ferries. I thought the sign *Tenez La Gauche* would make a good pseudonym, a bit like when Tony Hancock decided to use the name Melton Mowbray when he took up poetry in an episode of his TV series. The sun was out and the larks were singing high over the friendly stalls. It was a great day but some cloud was in me. I bought nothing.

I had begun to note what I didn't buy, so I did record that I left an odd volume of Lives of the Popes, in the old Bohn Classics series, which I like and have often bought. Later, I contemplated nothing. As boot sales were now a kind of work for me, I should always buy something, even if it was a small consumable. A boot sale is an exchange, so a token spend on one cheap thing should be a duty for good feeling. There may be a stop in your head, but the exchange must be made and the stroller thereby made good, made a part of a bigger whole. Especially on St George's Day, for the old poet of international and independent goodwill, Tenez La Gauche. Come on Tenez from Old School Road! Maybe I'd had too good a time buying old stop-watches and big old, confident books, earlier in the week. My timing was out.

No maps of Hertfordshire about. I was looking for them to try to visit some ancient yew trees, which are weird and timeless. Usually lots of old Ordnance Survey maps are about, now that people use the internet for navigation, for not knowing where the hell you are, but knowing the direction blindly. I liked old maps. You could see time on them, see the past. None were to be found this week, though. My navigation was a bit untimely that Friday.

I should have bought the Popes book. There was a Pope or two called Adrian, which might have been fun to read about. One of the good things about the internet is that you can find odd volumes, so I could have got volume I easily. I resolved to buy something, however small, in future. I thought of an old 78 record, bought a few years since, of Noel Coward, another great hero of that interwar period, reading Clement Dane's poem 'The Welcoming Land', and wondered where that spirit of open, positive Englishness had gone. Tenez La Gauche. Anyway, shopping is a sacred and timely thing, even a poetic thing, as I imagine G.K. Chesterton with a stop-watch, timing me as I choose something over nothing. I should have picked up on the sacred exchange.

As Chesterton's epic ballad is now out of copyright and also that England might find independence by proxy, I feel moved to include a bit of *The Ballad of the White Horse*.

This section, from 'Book I: the Vision of the King' is full of foreboding, where the landscape is haunted by giants from the past and a genuine sense of uncertainty about the future. These five stanzas, isolated in their stricter ballad-metre of four lines, stand on their own page, and immediately I read them they felt like a song. I might still make one of them.

Their souls were drifting as the sea,
    And all good towns and lands
They only saw with heavy eyes,
    And broke with heavy hands.

Their gods were sadder than the sea,
    Gods of a wandering will,
Who cried for blood like beasts at night,
    Sadly, from hill to hill.

They seemed as trees walking the earth,
    As witless and as tall,
Yet they took hold upon the heavens
    And no help came at all.

They bred like birds in English woods,
    They rooted like the rose,
When Alfred came to Atheney
    To hide him from their bows.

There was not English armour left,

    Nor any English thing,
When Alfred came to Atheney
    To be an English King.

If I do make a song, the last stanza here would be a chorus to the other verses and the title would be 'When Alfred Came to Atheney'. Chesterton, in his introduction, talks of tradition foreshortening and telescoping history. Tradition makes all things timely.

Week 3:
MAGIC AND MELANCHOLY

WEDNESDAY 28TH APRIL 2021. MARKS TEY.

A Book of Magicians. ed. Roger Lancelyn Green.

Twenty One Poems. Ruth Fainlight. (Signed first edition).

The Mabinogion. Folio Society.

Regeneration. Pat Barker.

Water Birds.

An Artist's Life. Alfred Munnings. (Book club).

All 50p.

THURSDAY 29TH APRIL. SKIP FIND, WIVENHOE.

Boat.

FRIDAY 30TH APRIL. HORSLEY CROSS.

The Anatomy of Melancholy (Volume 1). Robert Burton. 50p.

The Casual Vacancy. J.K. Rowling. £1.

SATURDAY 1ST MAY. WEELEY.

English Journeys. (Penguin; 20 vol. box). £2.

Frank Skinner on the Road. 50p.

The Best of S.J. Perelman. £1.50.

Looking back to last week's log, I had overlooked something added in pencil. The first things I saw, arriving at Marks Tey, were two old red mopeds, possibly Honda 50s, covered in dust and rust. People were photographing them. Was it because there were two? Collections of odd things being sold off at boot sales often make good photos. I've seen suitcases full of matchbox labels and a friend with me has photos of a box full of about 50 toast racks. My friend Sarah once bought a whole bin bag full of 1950s cheap costume jewellery, from which she made an artwork. I still have a pair of Bill Haley earrings she gave me when we sorted them out.

Sadly, however, my theme for this week ties in with what's happening in my life. Last Monday, the friend who first got me interested in magic died. Last Tuesday, the friend who taught me mythology at university died. It was always likely these two men, who didn't know each other, would come into this chapter, especially as one was mentioned in a book I'll cover. My own first creative writing book, *Myth and Creative Writing* (2011) was dedicated to "my myth teachers, Robert Hill, and Dudley Young, whether they like it or not". Their deaths ring with the kind of coincidence that both might have appreciated.

A Book of Magicians by Roger Lancelyn Green links me back to them also, as it does to Week One, with the same author. This book seems like an addition to the four books of his *Myths and Legends* box. My box of magicians is getting emptied into the sacred and I keep thinking of Henry Vaughan's old metaphysical poem: "They are all gone into the world of light! / And I alone sit ling'ring here..."

I have had a number of magical book appearances at boot sales. The first I remember is going to one on Chelmsford Race Course in the 1980s, for some reason with finding *The White Goddess* by Robert Graves in mind. Lots of magical Roberts. My pal Bob and Robert Bly come to mind. At Chelmsford, I seemed to plough through tons of useless trash-like books. The very last stall had the book I wanted, which I almost couldn't believe. I still have the book, and I see the race track was called the Essex Show Ground then. I bought the book for 30p on 24th of August 1986, naturally/ spookily one day after Dudley Young's birthday. It is still one of the defining books of literary magic.

I remember writing the chapter about the hero in *Myth and Creative Writing*. I went to Marks Tey. There I found Carlyle's lectures *On Heroes, Hero-Worship, & the Heroic in History* (1841), for 10p I think, from which I quoted. Carlyle pointed out that you had to have a heroic mind to see the heroic. I try to take these magical occurrences as normal, as I was taught by my friend Bob to develop a magical mindset. He had variously made a living as a clairvoyant and as a book dealer. He taught me to find books and the magical in the everyday. I remember him saying to me, "Either the universe has meaning or it doesn't." All things are connected, you could say, or magical connection is normal. This is connection by meaning rather than cause and effect, which is what synchronicity means.

When I finally went to university in my forties, Dudley

took over as my hero/mentor and great teacher – to go in my own book of magicians. He taught a class called Primitive Mythology, which was incredibly sophisticated, of course. I then took his third-year literature class. When I became a teacher myself, I had the equipment to go on from teaching myth and creativity into an advanced version at MA level, called Writing Magic. While I was devising this class and the book that came from it, *The Magic of Writing* (2018), the magical books seemed to jump into my hands. Planning a class on the trickster archetype, the definitive book on the topic, *The Trickster* by Paul Radin, appeared in the local Emmaus charity warehouse, for 50p.

About a year or two after this, maybe around 2015, I happened across a stall at Marks Tey which had so many magic and esoteric volumes, I could hardly choose how many I could carry. I went away with armfuls and kept going back. Every week they seemed to have more good stuff. All 50p for paperbacks and £1 for hardbacks. This was a stall run by two joking chaps, tricksters themselves. Incidentally, it was the same place I found the Chesterton biography, as if by magic, in Week 2.

One of the books I got there early on was about Carlos Castaneda. This was *Castaneda's Journey* (1977) by Richard de Mille. Dudley Young is mentioned in this. I knew Dudley had written about Castaneda and took with a pinch of salt his mumbled assertion that he had "made Castaneda famous" with his review. This is confirmed by de Mille. I found the review online – it was from the *New York Times Book Review*,

29th September 1968 and titled 'The Magic of Peyote'. This brought *The Teachings of Don Juan* to the attention of a big paperback publisher and thence fame, fortune and madness for Carlos. Reading *A Book of Magicians*, I wonder if Carlos was a classic sorcerer's apprentice, from Lucian of Samosata, unable to stop the magic he had started.

I bought dozens of books from the same stall over a few years. One notable one was by Madame Blavatsky and worth much more than £1. In 2019, when they seemed to be running out of the esoteric material, I asked the chaps where it had all come from. Their main things were antiques and they didn't seem to bother too much about the books, although both were witty and intelligent. I had a clue, as some of the earlier dated books had a name-stamp. I have one to hand, *Nostradamus* (1942), by James Laver, in a 1952 blue Penguin. 'J.A.G WHITE' is stamped on the white part of the cover, above the title, as well as inside, as if Mr White was trying out his stamp. My boot-sale chaps didn't remember the man's name but they told me it all came from the same place. The bookcases contained thousands of books in a maze-like room of bookcases, where you could hardly move between the shelves, the room was so packed.

Anyway, I bless my book magician, my White magician, student of the same things as me, who guided me like a cosmic librarian from beyond the grave in my passing on of some of his knowledge. And my two late magicians who died in sequence, last week, as I write. Thanks Bob, for getting me into magic and into finding books, and thanks White the book magician for giving me the gifts from beyond, and thanks to Dudley for his own books and influence. If I did my own book of magicians, I'd start here.

Roger Lancelyn Green's book is great I find, now that I'm reading it more closely. He was an interesting figure and a member of the Inklings with Tolkien and C.S. Lewis. He wrote novels too, and *A Book of Magicians* would have enhanced my chapter on Meeting the Magician no end. His book is scholarly and he retells and selects well. The world is awash with books about magic, as I used to tell my students in my Writing Magic MA class. Given this hugeness of the subject, its popularity and bibliography, I would get them to do presentations on something from their own interests. This was often the highlight of the 10 weeks of study, as some students, like Lou Hart, knew loads more than me anyway. Dudley Young came as a regular guest tutor and usually talked for two hours on Yeats, a dazzling feat of insight and intelligence, which reflected his first book, about Yeats, *Out of Ireland*.

Bob Hill had the touch with finding books, too. One day when visiting I found myself asking about the mystic Richard Gardner, who Bob had known. I had bought my paperback copy of his *The Tarot Speaks* in November 1974, many years before. At one point the next day, Bob returned from the town and had found copies of Gardner's other books, as if by magic, I think in a charity shop, which he then gave me. These were *The Purpose of Love* and *The Wheel of Life*, both good works on archetypes.

Dudley Young was more high culture, but his *Origins of the Sacred* is superb and made several books-of-the-year lists when it first came out in the 1990s. The paperback edition sold well. I've given several copies away but retain my own. Read it to change your way of thinking. Both these men could do that.

Bob used to joke that phrases in the Highway Code, the booklet you needed when learning to drive, had hidden significance. "Check for loose connections" was advice about looking under the bonnet. I do that all the time and now the connections seem strong.

Not strictly a boot sale, but with similar randomness, that week, was my finding a model boat in a skip. I had walked past the skip on my way to meet a PhD student Lelia in Wivenhoe. The skip had several models of boats in it. After our chat about her poetry, we walked back up the High Street, away from the estuary. I had told her about the skip. As we approached, there were two men standing by it. We stopped and talked.

One of them was clearing his father's house. His father had been a model boat builder and his grandfather, who had also lived there, had been a boat designer. This is not unusual for the still nautical town. The other chap turned out to be a fellow model boat man, who sadly had not known the other chap's father. I remarked that he was getting to know him now. The son told us we could take anything we liked, as the other chap was doing, as there were so many boats and he couldn't keep them all. Lelia took a plastic boat for her child and I took a hull, shaped by the grandfather, as part of a boat design. I loved the sea-shaped look of it, though I was not sure what I would do with such a thing. I ended up hanging it on the wall, beside some guitars. A little later I wrote a poem about the incident. I remembered talking to Dudley about Sutton Hoo (Wiven Hoo?) and him saying that they should have made more of the poetic side, citing a mutual favourite long poem, 'The Ship of Death' by D.H. Lawrence. My poem just tells the story, as simply as possible:

SHIP BURIAL

Wivenhoe isn't far from Sutton Hoo
and we found a kind of ship burial
in a skip

The history of the port was there –
the son of a model shipbuilder
whose grandpa had been a ship designer

Told the town's tale
as a place of ships and the dreamers
of ships

Another man talking to the son
who was trying to clear his Dad's house
turned out also to be a model shipbuilder

who never knew the deceased

'You're getting to know him now,' I said
and the good son gave us model ships
to take out from the skip
and carry away

I asked his Dad's name, as a small way of
honouring him, as we took and carried the ships onwards –
mine a hull of the grandfather's design
yours a model to share with your child

Carrying ships away to bless other lives
seemed like a dreaming kind of ship burial
a gift of baring up, and fluid imagination
or a model of a voyaging to some new life

Death calls to rebirth, via the bosom of the bigger world of the unformed, the sacred. My students were always interested in death and rebirth, curious to look these dark and serious matters in the face as well as they could, and stretch their imagination. I have always been too sentimental, or timid to be a magician myself but magic is a way into writing and wandering among books and boot sales.

On the Friday, I returned to my own taste of nothing bought at Horsley Cross. I went to the stall of a chap I often see there, who sometimes has a mess of books on the ground, often at 20p each, including some interesting or unusual stuff. Ah, another Bohn classic, of the same kind I overlooked last week. But this was Volume I, of three I think, of Burton's *The Anatomy of Melancholy*. I knew this was hard to find and usually expensive. A recent radio programme had examined this classic and the prices, even second hand of any condition, were too high. It is easily read online, but that's not the same. I paid my 50p without hesitation and asked if there were other volumes somewhere. There were not. Again, I thought I'd find the odd Volume II and possibly even Volume III to buy on the net. I found though that they were too expensive and that the one volume I had was going for £19. The book seemed to be addressing my nothingness of the previous week, just as it addresses the elegiac nature of these weeks.

I decided as I write to check online again. I found, yesterday, Volume II. The address of the seller is in Felixstowe. This is no distance from Horsley Cross, which is on the way to Harwich, where you can watch the big boats go into Felixstowe docks. Where, then is Volume III? It will sail to me eventually, I feel. I await Volume II, coming this week by post for a bargain £10. If I pay an average £5.25 a volume, I'm doing well.

Burton's early look into the dark of human souls was first published in 1620. I must have book-marked this passage, as it related to my work on poems from Ecclesiastes: "Self-love, pride, and Vain-glory... calls one of the devil's three great nets... Where neither anger, lust, covetousness, fear, sorrow...

nor any other perturbation can lay hold, this will slily and insensibly pervert us." This from part I, section II, subsect 14. Page 338 in my Volume I (Bohn's Popular Library, Bell and Sons, 1926).

Last week was my vanity, buying nothing, but I was having my lessons in losing my heroes, too. To shop, I noted at the time, you need to bring your imaginative sympathies with you, or let them awaken.

All is vanity, as Ecclesiastes says so many times. Maybe this is an act of vanity but my humble ambition has always been to align my life with my writing, without losing depth. I aspire to a kind of mythic or magic simplicity. Can I bring out the magic in the everyday, as Bob did, as Dudley Young did? I hope so. One thing to this point: I thought I was writing about then but I find I am also writing about now. This is inevitable and good.

Keen on my recovery from melancholy, Saturday found me at Weeley, where I found humour in Frank Skinner and S.J. Perelman and another boxed set. This time the box was torn and the books looked as if they would never fit in. The *English Journeys* set of 20 slim paperbacks was from Penguin in 2009. Some of it comprises sections from classic works of place and nature. Just the sort of reading I need for this project. The box does not have any curve or indentation for the fingers to extract a volume, so is poorly designed. I counted the books and got some into the torn box, but the set was only £2. They now go on the net for around £20.

Mending the box with a piece of strong, sympathetically coloured paper and PVA was easy. I pressed the books flat in my old heavy book press, as they seemed to have swollen a bit with damp, and it all went back together.

This ship of magic books now sits alongside Roger Lancelyn Green's box. I may cut some curved finger access to it, as even now they all fit, it is hard to get into. I must keep these magic ships afloat, for the "journey to oblivion", as Lawrence says in *The Ship of Death*.

Week 4: CROCKERY

WEDNESDAY 5TH MAY 2021. MARKS TEY.
Crown Ducal dessert bowl. 50p.

FRIDAY 7TH MAY, HORSLEY CROSS.
3 Heinz minestrone soup. £1.
Country Churches. Simon Jenkins. 50p.
Fungi. ZigZag book. 50p.

Crockery – what posh people call tableware. I love old crocks, being one myself. And I love this Crown Ducal dessert bowl, as listed above. I used it this morning for my porridge, as I do most mornings now since I found it in Marks Tey. The dish delighted me as soon as I saw it and I had some of the minestrone soup in it the next day for lunch. These are the small nourishing delights of the boot sale, even in lean weeks. Crockery and food. It's not always just about books.

In my twenties, in Braintree, I used to go to the market on Wednesdays, to chat to the man who ran the record stall. Later, he became the boss of a big record store chain in East Anglia called Parrot Records. I bought a folk album from him, second hand, probably by The Young Tradition, and subsequently we had a chat most weeks. There used to be crockery stalls at markets in those days, selling all kinds of miscellaneous stuff, some if it seconds. I had already found bone china tea-plates for 10p at jumbles, but I remember buying a Caius College dinner plate from the stall, probably a second. It had a black design on dull white ceramic and I used it till it got broken in the 90s.

There's a regular chap at Marks Tey, not there this particular week, who sells lovely old crockery, I think because he loves the stuff. I once told him that I tend to buy only one plate at a time, as I like to have them all different. He looked at me curiously and confessed he did the same.

Can I make an aesthetic of this? So, he likes old crocks – how surprising/ interesting? Well, it is something to do with not liking pure whiteness and not liking conformity, as well as not liking new things. Is not liking new things a posh or a poor thing? Obviously both, but it is also something to do with noticing stuff and not trying to dress a table, as in tableware, but somehow living more simply and deeply. My dad, God bless him, taught me not to care what people thought of you. I guess we were too bohemian to conform. Our crockery was promiscuous and I had my favourite mug and plate, as is natural with mostly inherited or donated tableware. The word makes me laugh.

Going back to collections of stuff being sold at boot sales (see Week 3), I'm sure my pal who liked photographing such things also had a snap of a box full of egg-cups. These smallest of crocks were a thing between us. She, having grown up in Canada and the States mostly, had no egg cups in the house. As many in a recent 'Twitter-storm' have found (I'm told), I also found this a strange deprivation, though not a cause of 'fury'. I wonder if the deprivations of World War II had made the ritual of the boiled egg such a thing, until recently I think, in England? My step-mum Betty used to crack an egg, pour it out, then chase the last bits of the contents out with her finger, so as not to waste a morsel. An egg was a precious thing in the war and I recently saw an old film where the gift of an egg from a woman to a man was precious too. The man placed the egg in his pocket. Later in the film, as they embraced, the eggs gets cracked. "Never mind, dear," says the woman, "we'll have it scrambled."

Listen to the song 'Hey Little Hen'.

I took delight in buying my pal a pair of vintage egg cups from a nostalgia-themed charity shop, and then making a ritual of us having a boiled egg with toast, marmite an option, which must be savoured slowly and eaten with a cup of tea to avoid the dryness of egg and toast. A nice small tea-spoon makes the ideal egg-spoon. She was bemused but went along with me. It was a sweet time. We discussed the slicing off of the top versus the tapping with the spoon. I told her that my dad used to alternately give my brother and me "the top off Daddy's egg" to eat. So I favour the slice. We discussed Jonathan Swift's *Gulliver's Travels*, where a war is described between the 'big-enders' and 'little-enders', who favour different entry points into the egg. I was reminded somehow of the EU arguments prevailing at the time. We are little-enders, I fear. Out of such jolly trivialities we wove a relationship I still miss. We took ages over breakfast, then went to Manningtree to go to the market, then walk the dog along the estuary and have fish and chips for lunch. Dear, departed days, however recent.

The crocks I buy are not usually valuable, but they are uniformly not white. The fashion for bright white I deplore, as it calls to an aesthetic of purity and unconsciously to a kind of white power, I believe. White van man has been replaced now by white car man and woman. Aggressive driving is their signature, these go-getters. It all reminds me of the white-lead women used to poison their faces with until recently, in the form of make-up. Greek statues were thought to be white when they were made, as they are today. We now know that they were painted colourfully and this white purity was never real, it was something recently made-up. I've never been married, but I remember in the late 1960s going to a wedding where the bride wore black and the groom a white suit – cool.

The Coronavirus pandemic might be called the White Death, as opposed to the Black Death of older days. It seems to be a disease of the rich, developed world and its urge is for a kind of universal uniformity. Have I gone too far? I hope so.

All this, just to justify the fact that I love old, cheap off-white tableware? Well, yeah. The soft-coloured background, the baskets of roses, the sheer variety of styles and patterns. J&G Meakin's universal pastoralism I love. The reason why you can buy Wedgwood plates for next to nothing is another white-goods invention. The name of this ghastly enemy? The dish-washer. Such old plates are not impervious to these machines' damaging attentions.

Aged 15, I once said to my Aunty Molly that washing-up is good for the soul. I could tune in to people even then and find the phrases. She never forgot it and I do still think I was right. How can we share such insights without doing the washing-up, or the dishes, as Americans would say? Aunty Molly and me were doing them. This convivial sharing, this cleaning, this ablution, this ceremony of water and domestic calm is vital to civilisation, it seems to me. The white-goods slave is no happy replacement. All you can share is arguments over how to stack it. Whatever way you stack it, it doesn't stack up. If you have a big family, it's fine, but I'm sure you also do a bit by hand now and again. This domestic baptism is vital to sanity. I love to wash my old, beautiful crocks and see the roses re-emerge like spring.

As a young man I worked in a Devon hotel, washing-up. Any cracked plates I used to save and put under my sinks. Then, when the waiting staff found any customers especially annoying, I would open the window above my sinks. Just a couple of yards opposite was a brick wall. Throwing a plate to smash against it was a great release for a tortured waiter. I would then go out with my big broom and sweep up. There was something of the fun and even homeliness in this service that still makes me laugh. We kept it secret from the manager, of course.

Now I save old crocs from oblivion but the weight of significance in an old plate transcends destruction. It is natural for youth to want new things that fit them better, but now the old things feel like they fit me in their call from other homes which found comfort in them.

I bought no jugs this year but I have a window ledge lined with nice old ones of no especial value. Two are Falcon Ware – one from my childhood and one bought recently for a pound. They both have water and bridges on them. A large and small jug with 'ladies' on them are also Falcon, I read.

Falcon ceased production in 1964 but their designs look older. There is a matching saucer to the smaller 'ladies' jug; all three bought on separate occasions. The whole line-up is eight jugs, never used but they look good to me. There's something useful in their shape, something made for the hand, made for pouring. Lemonade, home-made, or milk from your own small-holding. They have my childhood comfort in them I suppose, but they look floral and friendly, rustic and domestic in a way modern goods do not.

When I lived in Halstead, I had a huge teapot of blue enamel, bought from a jumble for a pound. When a pal and me wanted some beer to take away from the nearby Nags Head, I took it and got four pints in easily, to everyone's amusement. The carrying handle at the front helped me get it back home. I think I left this treasure behind, sadly. I have a smaller, similar one, but again I rarely use it. I admire the utility without the use. Is this wrong? I have had an old scoop for decades but recently started using it to weigh my porridge. It was last used for guinea pig food in the 80s and I'm glad I kept it. Cutlery I rarely buy, though I know spoons players who hunt for good items of electro-plated nickel silver (EPNS). I love the way cutlery accumulates and becomes various in drawers, from every era and person who left some. I suppose no-one leaves stuff in drawers anymore? Maybe they do. The hand-me-down world is under threat. All this led me to a poem celebrating the hand-me-down as a definition of tradition.

HAND-ME-DOWN

Hand-me down was all I had
In a poor family when I was a lad
Worn-out short trousers to my knees
A friend's old brogues, so kids could tease
I longed for the new they sold in town
When I wore that hand-me-down

For adolescents to want it new
Seems a natural thing to do
But I changed my point of view
About the old stuff and the new
Something knitted by my late mum I found
For my late dad – just a hand-me-down

A sign of riches not poverty
Were things that people gave to me
Even that peeling three-piece-suite
That stuck to your jumper when you left your seat
Take a piece of us with you, my wind-up wound
When they sat on our hand-me-down

Cutlery mingles in the drawer
From generations and folks before
New and old, they're just like us
All mixed-up, promiscuous
Like spoons – at it like knives all round
Shameless forkers, hand-me-downs

And now I treasure gifts passed on
My loud voice and eager tongue
My way in the world, my stance, my face
All that foolishness or grace
Passed down through to me, now resound
I call tradition hand-me-down

All my fathers, all my mums
All the sweet old songs that come
To my mind at every hour
Are tradition's perennial flower
All strength and love, any renown
It's all a kind of hand-me-down

If I could go back to my childhood clothes
I'd say you can't buy one of those
To reassure dad that it was ok
To dress a poor boy the old way
I'd give my thanks and make no frown
And celebrate the hand-me-down

Hand-me-down's not limiting
Like parents' love it's everything
Hand-me-down songs, hand-me-down shoes
Go round the town and spread the news
Let 'the oldest, yet the latest' sound
All your best lines are hand-me-down

On Friday at Horsley Cross, the fungi book looked unpromising from the outside, but it is a zig-zag book which opens out into a long line of vivid, saturated colour illustrations characteristic of the early 60s. I intend to put it on the long wall of the stairs.

My main plate buying that day is of large soup bowls, which coincides in my mind with making mushroom soup. I think I had some very mushroomy soup, definitely not 'cream-of' but dark and flavourful, in the antique centre in Priory Street. It was served in old, big soup bowls. Can you buy big soup bowls new? Not sure, but old ones are lovely and quite common. By now, I have quite a collection. The old antique centre has turned into accommodation, like so many good, old places.

I experimented to make such a soup for my old bowls. Eventually a mix of onions, fried with garlic and half the bag of dark mushrooms, then mixed with a bit of potato and mint and a vegetable stock-cube, along with the rest of the mushrooms, served to make a good big bowl full. I must do that soup again, maybe for my friend who used to like it, if she visits soon.

This week I had also been reading SJ Perelman's collection from last week. He was such a modernist, too far-out for our tastes maybe – surrealistic and neologistical. He wrote scenarios for the Marx Brothers and was highly praised in his day. I doubt anyone so experimental would be tolerated now, but he is bracing to read. And he gives you courage. I think that is what I buy for, at boot sales. It's that connection to the courage of the past.

The other book in the two-for-a-pound buy, with the fungi book, was a duplicate from the *English Journeys* series, about churches. This was a present for someone, as we will see in weeks six and seven.

Even a quiet week at the boot sales is good for these chipped and cracked thoughts, suddenly found sound and not thrown at the wall.

Week 5:
FATHERS AND SONS

WEDNESDAY 12TH MAY 2021. MARKS TEY.

2 78 records – one by 'Roy Leslie' and one written by Leslie Sarony. £1.

Medieval and Renaissance Music. David Munrow LP. £1.

A5 folder. 50p.

In Hazard. Richard Hughes. Penguin.

The New Forest.

Islands Round Britain. Britain in Pictures.

Rebels and Reformers.

Early Railways. King Penguin.

Coarse Fishing. (8 books.) £12.

The Modern Gift Book for Children. Odhams Press. £1.

SUNDAY 23RD MAY. ARDLEIGH.

Dear Life. Alice Munro. 50p.

3 post-it notes. £1.

3 O.S. maps, including Herts. £2.

Leather belt. £1.

A busy, sunny day on the Wednesday and the find that cannot be overlooked is the 1948 Odhams Press *The Modern Gift Book for Children*. This book has a story in it by my dad, John May, and one by my granddad, Bert May. Dad's story is 'The Kitten That Whispered'; Grandpa's is 'The Hookey Stick'. My Dad had worked for Odhams Press as a journalist/general writer. They were a big publisher at the time, given to cheap self-help books and compilations like the one I found for £1.

Dad told stories about working there. He remembered the firm writing to George Bernard Shaw to suggest doing an omnibus edition of his works. The letter was in glowing terms of praise for the great man. G.B.S. sent back a postcard which simply read, "Cut the cackle. How much? G.B.S." Dad says he wished he had stolen it when he left.

What he did steal however was a lovely antique chair he used in the office. This had a high back and curved wooden armrests. Apparently, the boss of Odhams saw Dad loading this into his car on the day he was leaving. "What are you doing with that chair, John?" came the question. "Stealing it," Dad replied, which he then did. He always used it.

My dad had encouraged his own dad to write a story, as Bert was very creative. He was a choir-master, pianist, composer and artist. He was also a bit daft in his humour and had a loud voice. I remember him singing 'Widdecombe Fair', in slow, tremulous cadence and it going on for ever. I feel that I might be more like him than I am my dad, but with less talent. It is hard to tell when you are close.

My dad John took a pseudonym for his name, John Dewey (his mother's maiden name), while Herbert used his own. Sometime my dad was dismissive of his own, less ambitious dad, but the creativity of Bert was never in doubt. As I write, on St Edmund's Day towards the end of November, I am looking at two carols they wrote together. Bert wrote the music, John the words.

Bert lacked ambition, unlike John in his thrusting world of journalism and manly joshing with the boss. In that way, I'm surely more like Bert. Friends would say I'm a bit unworldly. I still have a few of my grandpa's books. His old Penguin Classic of Sophocles' *The Theban Plays* with its tale of Oedipus still sits within reach. My mum died when I was young and my dad blamed himself, at least for a while, though it was no-one's fault. My own psychology might be there somehow in that text and these facts. What one finds are not mums so much as dads at boot sales. There are women, of course, but it is mostly men and often their stuff for sale. Are women perhaps not so accumulative? I look for my mum among the music, but mostly find my dad.

All our dads are there – all their sheds, all their dreams, all their works, their work, their lost collections, their hopes and their ruins. On Wednesday, at Marks Tey, I find my music-hall hero first. I met Leslie Sarony when I was in my late twenties and he was in his eighties. He recorded many 78s and I've been collecting them for more than 40 years and still find ones I've not got. He was the great songwriter/ performer who wrote 'Ain't It Grand to be Bloomin'

Well Dead' and 'Jollity Farm'. I wrote a song about him, interviewed him, saw him live recording a TV show and have performed songs of his including 'Don't be Cruel to a Vegetabuel' (sheet music bought at a boot sale, of course). I have a signed note from his on the wall of my living room. Funny, lively, silly, professional and prolific, he was like a cross between my dad and granddad. I'm not as funny as him, or anywhere near as successful, but he was to me like Muddy Waters might have been to the Rolling Stones. The King of English Song, as well as the King of Comic Song, as I called him in my tribute song. 'I Lift Up My Finger and I Say... Tweet-Tweet, Hush-Hush, Now-Now, Come-Come...' as he said.

Both my mother's and father's families were musical and liked comic songs. Bert used to write comic songs for his firm's outings. One, when they were going to the Crooked Billet, Waltham Abbey, for a lunch celebration, went: "Let's all go down to the Billet / Come and don't question me why / Open your mouth and we'll fill it / With pie, pie, pie." I know the tune too, but not the verses to which this was the chorus. It was passed down to me in the traditional way, by my dad, from his dad.

My mum was a pianist. She used to sit outside the music shop opposite the Regal in Edmonton and demonstrate sheet music on the piano. She also used to accompany her dad, Dick Gilks, singing comic songs in Buffalo Lodges. Many of the folk clubs I've played are in rooms which were old Buffalo Lodges. I'm very much a traditional singer, ukelele player (Mum played uke) and songwriter. My recent work on tradition talks of this, as does the following song of recent composition, which is fiction for two verses, then all true. It uses the old image of tradition, that of a tool being the same, while renewed in parts. The oldest, yet the latest thing, as Ray Noble wrote.

MY GREAT GRANDPA BOUGHT A SPADE...

My great grandpa bought a spade
    Solid and English made
It's had 12 new handles and 10 new blades
But it's still the same one he displayed
When my great grandpa bought a spade
    Great Grandpa bought a spade

My great grandma made some wine
    She made it strong and fine
She used old bottles that still are mine
It tastes as it always did – divine
When my great grandma made some wine
    Great grandma made some wine

Both my grandfathers sang a song
    Comic, wide and long
The same but different and just as strong
As I do now and carry on

As when my grandfathers sang a song
    Both grandfathers sang a song

My mother played the ukulele
    She held it like a baby
And now that baby is old and flabby
And now he holds the ukulele
The same as Mum played like a baby
    That little ukulele

My old dad he wrote a poem
    Wrote it like his home
And I am keeping that poem going
And this is the same one he was crowing
When my old dad he wrote a poem
    My dad he wrote a poem

This song is just goes round and round
    Banal and yet profound
It's something to do with spiritual health
If you want any more you can sing it yourself
It goes around like a kind of wealth
    So you can sing it yourself

My great grandpa bought a spade -
    Solid and English made

This song goes to a Morris style tune and we get people to

pretend to do Morris hand movements when we do it. My bassist partner Murray Griffin said, first time out, it looked like exercise time in an old people's home. It was exactly like that.

The Modern Gift Book for Children is good and I feel I have left it hiding in plain sight. Both my dad's and grandpa's tales are magical again. Magic is for children but also for thinking in ancestral terms. One thing I did look at and used to have a photocopy of, on my wall at work, is the frontispiece illustration, in full colour. It is a painting by Blanche Sinclair called 'Salubrious Place', which has a lovely lack of conventional perspective, with ships going uphill in a Cornish scene reminiscent of the kind of primitive (so-called) art of Alfred Wallace. It is a beautiful, bright thing of magical intensity. Its caption refers you to a story *The Spriggan of St Ives* by Eileen Molony. The story is set in St Ives and I wonder if the two, illustrator and author, were from there and knew each other. It is a magical story of artists and a supernatural fairy-like creature, the titular Spriggan.

I rarely read children's books as a child, seeming thirsty for realism, as many kids are. Now I look on them in real wonder at the magic allowed. In fiction the generations join in a world which is more magical than the reality they lived somehow. This was where the gentle world of silliness and the grim business world were aligned, where my struggles with the meaning of masculinity found its answer in the least likely place.

I thought the Roy Leslie 78 was really Leslie Sarony using one of his many pseudonyms to make more records. One play told me it wasn't him. Sarony had a high, distinctive voice, instantly recognisable to a fan like me. I find it is actually his partner Leslie Holmes. Holmes was a music publisher, pianist and songwriter who formed the duo with Sarony in 1935 called The Two Leslies, which lasted till 1946. They had some hits together. The two sides feature the same song, which is another version of the popular joke form, an example of which might be 'She was only a post-master's daughter, but o how she sorted the mails'. This is another instance of the two Leslies being close to folklore and popular sayings. I have somewhere another tune with such formed rhymes. Sarony made a disc called *Rhymes*, which consisted of limericks to music. Holmes's song is 'She was Only a Postmaster's Daughter, But...'

The other is also a 9" Eclipse, featuring the song 'Sing Holly! Go Whistle! Hey! Hey!' This is by Malcolm Desmond, of whom I've not heard, but many recorded this Sarony song from the early 1930s. His songs are adaptable and any of the now non-PC verses could easily be rewritten. I myself wrote an extra verse or two for 'Mucking About the Garden' and 'Don't be Cruel to a Vegetabuel'. The latter included the lines, "The organic Prince of Wales / Always sings this to the snails."

Sarony was, it seems, an intense, professional polymath of the music hall and people found him irritating. His son said his songs were 'trivial'. I disagree and feel he transcended his time. He was dancer, singer, comedian, actor and songwriter. He was also vulgar, trivial, broad and impressive. I liked him and, when I met him, thought he seemed complete. There are quite a few clips of him on the internet and he seems to me original and to have a timeless quality.

The Eclipse small 78s are often of folk-dance tunes and comic songs. These small discs have smaller sleeves round the hole. Because of this, they are rejected by my record player about 20 seconds before the songs' end. I love the labels of 78s. They often show the names of old record and music shops from the past, some of which I even remember. These places for dreaming men, like Hedley V. Norfolk in Braintree and Saville Pianos in Ilford, I seem to remember. But the one I have advertising Morton J. Root's shop in Halstead was long gone before my time. These were often big places, full of instruments and activity. I think of my mum playing the piano outside such a shop and my grandpas buying comic-songs 78s.

They were not all as serious as my dad. I seem to have been in retreat from serious men all my life and I feel now, at boot sales like this, I am approaching their secret frivolity, as personified by Leslie Sarony and the old, dreaming worlds of music. Are women more sensitive to the silliness of men than other men? I have usually found it so. My book of poems and songs called *Comedy of Masculinity* (2014) talks about this and an earlier poem sees my dad like the invisible old oak the road still goes round.

THE BOHEMIAN SWERVE

My dad was a semi-recluse
   down a long lane lived he
The lane was straight until it swerved
   around an old oak tree

My dad was hard to get around
   firm and fast as oak
and people tell me I'm the same
   and I can take a joke

My dad was a poet, a singer
   like his dad before and me
That's the way we have to swerve
   to see things differently

Now I'm grown up and my dad has gone
   and the oak tree's long gone now
though the same long lane still swerves
   around it anyhow

It's my bohemian inheritance
   to stand half-distantly
to sing and swerve around these things
   like an old oak tree

And I am both the oak and swerve
   paradoxically

I move and am moved like a dance
  a bit mysteriously

No nearer or straighter will I go -
  Tradition you can't see
is individuality
  for my dad, his dad and me

The past is written through us
  I take it seriously
Related, recalled, known, unknown
  the deep world walks with me

Down the long lane with my song
  I swerve mysteriously
in roots and strength and new green leaves
  around the invisible tree

This lyric is from my *Ballads of Bohemian Essex* (2011) and I was reminded of it by an old pal who wrote to me about having felt it chime with him of late. I see that father figures have always been big with me. I now recall other finds of my father's work at boot sales. I have some *Eagle* annuals he contributed to, some *John Bull* magazines from the 1950s. One set of books he wrote many of, having taken the project over from another journalist, was one given away free by the *Daily Herald*, published again by Odhams Press and called

Live Successfully. Dead serious. I bought a set in their original packaging and I1/2d stamp from a second-hand stall in Halstead market in the 1980s. I saw another set holding up the broken leg of a friend's sideboard in the 1960s – so many thin books made a good way to build something supporting at precisely the right height. Very dated, I am sure some of it is sound advice and some not at all what we would read today without self-important disapproval. I might not buy another set, even if I saw one. They don't have his name on them, even though I think he wrote all of them from number two, which he finished for the other journalist, onwards.

I notice that number one of these books was posted in 1938 and I can't help but wonder if the Leslies read them when they went solo. I can't emphasise how alien these self-help things would have been to me when young. The seriousness of these manly views of capitalism made me sick and I lacked all conviction. It was the exuberant triviality of the music hall – and of Sarony especially – I saw as subversive.

I imagined these books to be worthless but a quick check finds a set of 16 for sale on the internet for £70, which seems a hopeful price at best. I have only 13 and got the impression from my dad that they had stopped with the coming of the world war in 1939. Now tempted to find the missing three but also wondering if they were written by someone else at Odhams. I think my dad's original copies amounted to 13 too.

On the Sunday, I went for the only time that year, as it

turns out, to Ardleigh. Ardleigh's is a big boot sale but one less interesting to me than Marks Tey as it has fewer house clearance chaps. The Alice Monro stories I found, however, were brilliant, full of sensitive portraits of men and women, as a counterbalance to my thoughts of my own troubled and inspired father figures. The waywardness of the human spirit is often her subject.

And a note to self: I should go more often to Ardleigh's boot sale as it is more working-class in flavour and some good finds are there. One stall holder, of my own generation I think, was shouting, "All stolen; have a look!" He got plenty of laughs. The cheerful rebellions of the ordinary man appealed to me as being nuanced and friendly, both silly and mocking in the best way. Alice did the complications too. This book I read straight away on my return home.

Making connections in time seems to be a feature of boot sale musings and finding evidence of times connected to you somehow seems to transcend time. This same week, I thought again of my 'swerve' poem. This was in connection to oaks in general. They signify fathers. My friend James Canton's *The Oak Papers* (2020) comes to mind. When I visited James' house, I noticed he has a desk like one I have at home, in oak with distinctive drawers. A lovely honey-coloured oak, his has the roll top; missing from mine. They both were owned by our fathers. The solidity and glow of fathers is both a good thing and something to swerve round.

Realising that some of my own serious writing comes from

these various father figures, I thought of another song lyric. It is perhaps the darkest song from my *Comedy of Masculinity* and attempts to show the rift between the generations we felt in the 1960s, I think. Echoing Turgenev's *Fathers and Sons* and Brel's lyric to the song 'Sons of'.

SONS AND FATHERS

Sons of chauvinistic swine
Sons of fascists, we were thine
Sons of bleak authority
Sons of violence, emotion free
     Sons of men who couldn't speak
     Sons of strong disguising weak
     Sons of intellectual scorn
     Sons not asking to be born

I miss my father, even when he was still there
I miss my father, pretending that he didn't care
Sons and fathers stumble towards each other in the dark
Saying who the hell are you

Sons of monsters you repressed
Sons of secretly depressed
Sons of moral hypocrites
Sons of poison acid wits
     Sons of job security
     Sons of the soul's penury

Sons of leave the rich to rob
Sons of only doing my job

Sons of racist homophobes
Sons of sons who stole the globe
Sons of torturers and worse
Sons of sins of fathers' curse
    Sons of bullies, bullied too
    Sons of men we never knew
    Sons of being right and safe
    Sons of cannon-fodder's graves

Sons betrayed without a kiss
Sons sold out to industries
Sons of the polluted river
Sons of nuclear end forever
    Sons who feel they've failed their mother
    Sons who cannot help each other
    Sons of sell the national health
    Sons of don't have kids yourself

O my father, listen to my prayer
O my father, sometimes you're still here
All the good in you I saw, are all the things the world ignores
Daddy so I hardly knew
Sons and fathers stumble towards each other by and by
Asking who the hell am I?

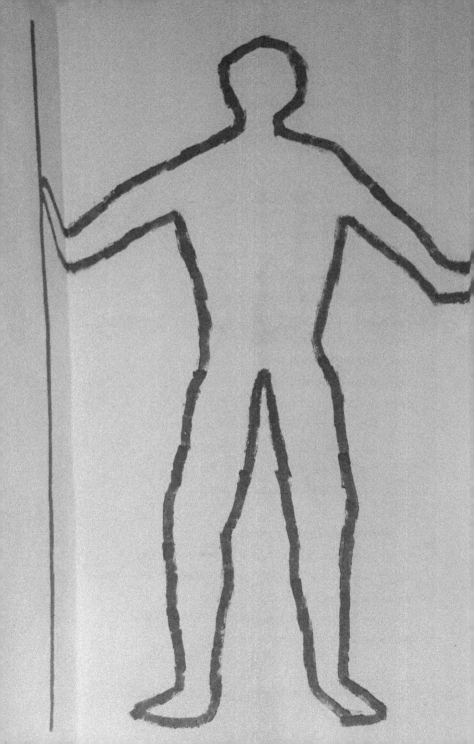

Weeks 6 and 7: GIFTS

WEDNESDAY 25TH MAY 2021. MARKS TEY.

A Local Habitation. Norman Nicholson.

1000 US Poems.

Nice Work. David Lodge. (3 for £2).

The Tailor of Panama. John Le Carre. 50p.

Goodtime George CD. George Melly. 50p.

2 George Formby 78s. £2.

WEDNESDAY 2ND JUNE, 2021. MARKS TEY.

History of Essex. A.C. Edwards.50p.

The Outing. Dylan Thomas.

The General in his Labyrinth. Gabriel Garcia Marquez.

Inn Signs. Shire book.

The Canterbury Tales. Chaucer, 2 cassettes. 50p.

3 hand sanitisers. £1.

Post-it notes. 50p.

How to Draw Comics. £1.

Variety Songs. £1.

From the lists that start these chapters, you may have noticed that I buy quite a few books that aren't mentioned in the write-ups that follow. Many of these books go to the best bookshop in my area, as gifts for my pal Dave Charleston, poet and bookman. As I have said, boot sales are not for me predominantly about money, although it may be for some. These might be the early birds who come to glean the best stuff in an unseemly rush. But the whole vibe of the thing is more about exchange and feels celebratory at best. Good humour is universal at boot sales. These are gifts. It is a gift to the self to go there, even on a dull, muddy day like the first Wednesday above, in the last week of May, or a too-hot blaze of a day like the first one in June.

Of the items listed above, Dylan Thomas' little book went to my niece, who read its short text in one and enjoyed it. The George Melly CD was a cheap throw together of his early stuff which provided the soundtrack for my friend Murray, who was reading Melly's autobiography, including the timeless classic of a band on the road 'Owning Up'. The drawing comics book went to my pal Lance, whose PhD was about that art form and had seen it but didn't have his own copy. Many of the rest went to Dave for sale in Stoke-by-Nayland at the Open Road Bookshop. The gifts give me great pleasure if I find they are appreciated.

The gifts to myself are always there too. Stationery is always something I look out for. Of the two George Formby 78s, one was broken but the other was an obscure song I'm glad to have. Do De O Do / Chinese Blues are not the best but fun. The other one looks like it has a bite out of it, but you can still play the remaining bit. There is a radio repeat on later today about how George Harrison liked George Formby. I reckon Ravi Shankar told him to look in his own back yard too, in the go abroad to find news of home way that wise men tend to impart. Formby keeps cropping up and he's very Lancashire and very like his dad, droll and an amiable loser of the positive kind. He was also an awesome uke player. Not my hero but you cannot ignore him if you are interested in the old comic songs. The book of variety songs is another gift of the old stuff that is my education. It is the songwriters I admire above all, with their skill and poetic gifts. What might they write today, those great writers for Formby like Clifford and Giffe and Jack Cottrell?

There's a terrible virus sweeping the land
Called ukulele-21
Everyone is learning, a small thing in their hand
I wish they'd never begun
They all play so limply, if you know what I mean
You need a jab of Formby as a vaccine
Then maybe this virus would be more fun
Ukulele-21

The *Inns...* book and the Essex history are useful for research for other writing projects but I had most fun discussing US poetry with Dave when I gave him the old paperback anthology. Carl Sandburg came up and he rarely does these days. These paths to conversations open up and friends are summoned from these solitary wanderings. All roads lead from the boot sale.

The largest gift I ever gave was a semi-solid double bass case. These are so huge, sarcophagus-like and unless you are gigging and have a big van, useless except for the gag of lying in it. In fact, I knew someone who had thrown his brand-new case away, as he had nowhere to store it. Double basses tend to live in corners but spare corners are not all that common. Maybe it was my other pal's old new one.

I waited until near the end of the boot sale, when I knew the seller would be desperate to rid himself of the great black thing. If it's a tenner, I'll buy it, I said to myself. It was and I did. Murray, my pal and double bassist, sold it when he replaced his old double bass with a new one. 'Double bass with case' sounds good in an advert, even if what you get an encumbrance. Ladies and gentlemen, Murray Griffin on the encumbrance. It was a good, fun thing to buy to give. Boot sales can afford and forgive their frivolity. You can buy and give on a whim, but they are a repository of the strangely useless and the usefully strange.

There are some little cocktail forks from, I think, the 1950s, usually in a little display box, called 'Little Forks'. I bought some on a whim for Sarah, my artist friend from Dovercourt. She liked them and put them on display in a cabinet with a glass front, full of unusual objects, in her kitchen. We bought a few more sets of them in the next year or so. Those little forks said love. Now every time I see a set, I feel a little fork of regret in my heart that I haven't seen Sarah for so long. Sweet, shared things. Now I wander alone, wistfully sometimes among the festive junk and old treasures. I still have something you gave me displayed and imagine that your little forks still make you think of me. Love tokens, not to be used, except in their whimsical absurdity to remind us of a shred of sensibility. Sarah bought me a tiny wooden ball, with a face and wire arms and legs like a wood-sprite, for luck, and I still have it in reach now, tied by a ribbon through its loop to my Anglepoise lamp, also bought at boot sale of course. It smiles at me. I look for the priceless in the priced, I suppose, and our togetherness was beyond price. What price little forks now? I do see them occasionally on stalls but pass by, wistfully.

In Week 13 I bought a fiddle which looked promising. This was a gift to my niece. It was the most expensive thing I bought that year but I think it is actually worth a lot more, even if it is just her reserve violin for now. During the Covid pandemic, instruments were always few and far between. I think it was because of the various restrictions that kept people at home. Perhaps people took up their instruments. Or their ukuleles. But it may be that the generation who played are dying off and when their houses are cleared they are already free of such old-fashioned things. TVs took over. The gifts of age are about us and, in my case, within us.

Age is time to meditate, time to wander among the archival world of self and see what still shakes with wonder. Going to boot sales is trying to accept the pastness of the past and my slow wonder is a gift to me.

In the cold now, as I write, I think of my old teachers again and their devotion to poetry. In his time at the University of Essex, Dudley Young wrote a book about Yeats and Yeats' poems on age are sometimes funny and often brave, but dark too. T.S. Eliot's view of age was darker still, his 'gifts' of age were painful. I am an old thing among old things and now not even among them so much as among the archives of old things I have created.

Yeats' 'The Circus Animals' Desertion' is devastating, its gift being dark humour, I think. The poem begins with a search for inspiration, which is often there in Yeats' poems, especially the later ones. The eloquence about trying is part of his triumph, of course, and the image of the 'circus animals' as his gifts is both touching and absurd and a call to be content with his limits. This poem about diminishment is actually a tour de force. The second part of the poem reviews his career in a kind of confessional tone, saying he was concerned with surfaces. The third part is most devastatingly concerned with the sordid nature of what remains, the rubbish, although he does not use that exact word. There must be a kind of acceptance here, as he is talking about love and about the heart at base. There is a gloomy feel to this acceptance, however transcendent the language becomes.

I have been reading Yeats to find a poem to read at Dudley' Young's funeral, as his first book and love was Yeats's poetry. Dealing with the decadence of our times is a role of the poet/prophet, as Dudley said. My own feeling about the rubbish of life and its confrontation are gentler and less apocalyptic and might befit a lesser poet. I felt moved to reverse part III of the poem into a positive view of 'the rag-and-bone shop'. The lines echo, in reverse, Yeats' last eight lines:

The jolly junk shop of the heart
Is where my bike and ladders start
These reaching images not gone
They reach beyond the money slut
Old vessels, old bottles and a broken can
To festive stalls, junk in a street
To remind us where we all began
Celebratory, incomplete

Like all great writers, Yeats makes you want to write, which might not always be a good thing, as you risk a damning contrast with a master. He writes about writing often and his ambition and craft being questioned are central to his art and his times. His poems scan time and have large scope, where mine, if even worthy of discussion, are on a small scale.

Wandering among the junk
I do not seek significance

rather the acceptance of the ordinary
delight to be found in a shared field.

In the cool of now, winter store –
Low sun, frost on cars
offers no convivial gift
except a hiding, a waiting
thinking of a warmer world
where gifts counted
and kindled into song

I did buy a ladder at the boot sale, some years' back. My deep stair-well needed redecorating and I had looked at hiring a long ladder, which seemed to cost about £100, even then. I gave the chap 10 pounds' deposit and he promised to deliver it to get the balance of £25. Sarah said, "He's been taking 10 pound deposits all morning!" We laughed but he did arrive in the afternoon. I kept the ladder and used it again recently to paint my green giant.

My bike too came from a boot sale. I wanted an old bike that no-one would steal. This still works well. The alternative is to have the best bike you can buy and also have good insurance against theft. I chose the cheaper route. I cycle most days along the Colne near where I live. My transports are cheap but they work in the small fairground of my own heart and restart me often in my humble task. These again are gifts to the self that seem to me ones that threaten no reality in the rip-off world but enhance because of their ordinariness.

Occasionally I find things people are after. My pals John and Sue asked about my lovely big soup plates, so I got them two. "Will Royal Worcester do?" I asked them, as I handed them the £1-each bargains, in a Harrod's carrier bag, given by another stall-holder. My brother regularly placed orders with me, including replacing his loaned and never returned *Reader's Digest Repair Manual*, which is still a great classic for any householder. I easily found one for him. These are one among few Reader's Digest books worth seeking. Another one among many worthless is the brilliant *Folklore, Myths and Legends of Britain*, from 1977, often found for a quid and worth £8–10 at least. I have one with a dust jacket – really rare. There's several for £60–75 on the internet and one for just £1. Also one over £90. My experience is that a book shop might stretch to a tenner, but it is a good book. No author is listed, as is their policy, but one look at the small print of contributors, such as Katherine Briggs and Geoffery Ashe, tells you this is a still the best book on the subject and a great one for writers.

Reader's Digest were strange. I remember my dad telling me they didn't pay well. As a freelance writer, he had an interview with the editor once, who served him tea in a very small cup, while the boss had a giant one. "Mind you don't drown in that cup," my dad told him gently as he left. He was never asked to write for them again. Later, a piece he wrote was accepted and fact-checked practically to death in the US manner of those days. He later noticed that his 10 bulleted points in the article amounted to 11. His examples of amusement at their working methods continued then, over many years. Another legend of many stimulating ones.

When I take books over to Dave's shop, we often discuss values and try to catch each other out. Another gift to myself, and best book of the year a couple of years ago, was a first edition of *Rewards and Fairies* and one of *Puck of Pooks Hill* by Rudyard Kipling. The stall-holder demanded £4 each for the two. I told him I normally only paid £1 at boot sales and thus beat him down from £8 to £4 for both. *Rewards and Fairies* turned out to be worth quite a bit. After looking it up I realised why. It was the first publication of the poem 'If'. This is actually a masterpiece, overlooked because of its ubiquity, rather like *The Bible*. This was my book of the year. I gave away my old copies of these two books and kept the firsts, as they are nice volumes. Kipling is easy to find at boots, often in leather-bound copies. His books went to many editions, so they are rarely worth much, hence my hard bargaining.

Dave and I have fun guessing value before looking books up, just like we used to do in the old charity shop. You have to take internet prices with a pinch of salt and its best to look at what is sold or completed on eBay especially, so as not to get over-excited about made-up values. Books seem more and more about gifts of lost significance to me and less and less about actual money. It is not the book itself, it is the finding of the book and the finding of significance, of real value.

The classic book for writers on 'gift culture' is Lewis Hyde's *The Gift* (1983). Suitably I got a US Vintage paperback copy from a charity shop for 49p in 2002. I only know this as the original receipt is still in it. Hyde tells the old story of the pipe of peace being a pass-it-on gift with a value beyond its value as an object. Even antique shows on TV talk of someone else enjoying an item when people decide to sell. Anyway, this is a book I have often recommended to students and others. It has been republished often after Margaret Atwood said it was a favourite of hers to give away. His other book on tricksters is excellent too. I was delighted to find he is also a poet and creative writing teacher. I have a middle name the same as his and where I live begins with 'Hy'. This is the way meandering writers think.

After telling Dave about my magic chapter of this book (Week 3), and giving him a couple of bags of general stock, he offered me another Puffin. Charles Causley's *The Puffin Book of Magic Verse* (1974) is another 1970s classic I didn't know about and wish I had had when writing my own *The Magic of Writing*. The intro alone is superb, as it begins 'All poetry is magic'. Are all boot sales magic? Not exactly, but they can be.

Buying an old fishing book for poet and fishing author Chris McCully is bound to be a treat, as it is an excuse to meet and put academia and the world of poetry to rights. We had offices next door to each other for many years and now have to find time for our casual conversations about poetry, so much enjoyed but somehow taken for granted. Buying a book of Stevie Smith poems (see Week 17) for any female acquaintance who doesn't have one is more of a mission to spread her fame as a brilliant poet. I must have bought at least half a dozen over the years to give away. She has a particular charm and somehow the small world of boot sales and old songs would appeal to her, somehow like the cat in 'The Galloping Cat', who likes to 'gallop about doing good'. Her eye for telling detail and lyrical tender sympathy for the human condition make her ideal to find, ideal to give as a gift. I told the stallholders about my mission and they thought I did it to seek a girlfriend. Not really so, though it might help. But a gift is a gift, no more and no less. Boot sales are no threat to your riches but they do challenge the world of getting and spending into a gentler and more human exchange, where the gift is beyond mere economics. Books, especially, do not say 'buy me', but 'read me', which is altogether different.

Week 8: MUSIC

WEDNESDAY 9TH JUNE 2021. MARKS TEY.

Folk Music Journal 1975. 50p.

Selected Poems. Ted Hughes. £1.

Grandma's Herbs. £1.

Record case. £5.

12" tom tom drum. £10.

It was hot this week and I didn't find much to buy I hadn't seen before. Boot sales can become becalmed mid-season, when there seems to be not much new. Out of the five items listed above, three are books and three are also directly related to music. If one wrote a song about herbs and set one of Ted's poems to a tune, all of them could relate to music. I'd also chatted to the stallholder with the old *Folk Song Journal* about local folk clubs, and talked with a local concertina player of note, who mocked me by asking if I'd had a "Don't you know who I am?" moment with the folk seller, which made me laugh.

Musical items are a big part of why I go to boot sales. Once, in the early 2000s, I was delighted to find a stall full of musical instruments, especially banjo ukuleles. I had been looking for one of these and came up to the stall as a man named Dave was demonstrating one to a potential customer. He was a cheerful looking man in a blazer and he could really play – he was doing the famous Formby 'split-stroke' playing style, which I am still unable to do. We talked and I said I wanted to buy one but didn't have the cash and wasn't sure which to buy. He gave me his phone number and said I could come round to see his banjo ukes at his house, as he had others that he could sell, including a small-bodied one of the kind I was after.

I tend only to buy something musical when I identify a need for it, except for bargains at boot sales. That is my rule but I do break it now and then. I was thinking of trying to record my song 'Everyone's Drunk In Essex' and felt I needed a banjo uke to do some light, driving rhythm in an overdub. My excuse.

Dave gave me instructions to find his place, two or three miles away, out near Great Bromley. He leant me a banjo uke and eventually I bought a good quality Dallas model from him, probably dating from the 1950s. He told me what I really needed was a UB1, a Gibson model, sometimes called a Baby Gibson. These are small, well-made and very loud.

Although about eight years older than me, Dave and I had lots in common. We both loved boot sales and instruments. We had both grown up in the countryside of Essex. Although I was a university lecturer, we were both autodidacts, though he might not have used the term. We both had a penchant for old songs, nature, bargains and the kind of gentle humour of the English workman. Before Dave retired and I belatedly entered academia, we had both had 'ordinary' jobs.

The kind of intellectualism that tends to be rife at universities was not really ever to my taste. To me as a writer and songwriter, the heart is more important than the head. Dave was the perfect antidote to the kind of people I was among most days. He was funny and wise and a decent old independent man. We found we had both lived in Braintree at the same time but had not met, though he knew my busker band-mates from the time, as he had been a railway man. I'd done lots of normal jobs too in the past. It didn't take us long to become best mates.

I remember talking to Dudley Young, author of the awesome *Origins of the Sacred* with its mix of myth, good sense and poetic insight. I told him I sometimes described myself as the university literature department's "token anti-intellectual". He said, "I describe myself as post-intellectual," adding, "You can have that one for free." Ukulele Dave was a great companion, full of songs and stories and the perfect antidote to the department. He also liked to hear a new song, especially on the uke.

I had recently taken to playing the uke more. It was a big part of my act early on as a folk artist, as its comic potential broke up the more serious guitar-based songs I performed. It also carried an intended flavour of the variety stage. No-one was playing the uke in those days, so I was different. I remember a traditional musician asking me how I'd come to play it. I told her there was always one around at home and that my mum used to play. She told me I was a traditional ukulele player. I was delighted.

Now that the uke was becoming more uke-biquitous I had decided to show these Johnny-come-ukulatelys how to do it. This was playing in English tuning, a tone higher than the usual US tuning that most players use now, and played aggressively in Formby style or, like I did, a more skiffle-based style with a plectrum. I still had my old Aloha Royal wooden uke, bought for £8 at Epping Flea Market. Solid mahogany and loud. Dave liked my stuff and was always keen to hear me. I now realise I started writing more for the uke, partly to entertain him. It was worth making him laugh.

Dave had some lovely ukes, especially a Ludwig Wendall

Hall and a nice little koa wood one, which must date from the 1920s at the latest, as it has porcelain machine heads. It is made in the USA and cost him £4 at a boot sale. We went to the Ukulele Society of Great Britain's biannual meetings together. I'd never been before and relished the wonderful mix of awful and brilliant and the tea and sandwiches of the old village hall variety. Wall-to-wall eccentrics, like us. It was on the way back from one of these meetings, having learnt the word 'plonkers' for uke players (as they go 'plonk-plonk' on the uke) I came up with the line "All my friends are plonkers and all their dogs have fleas". "My Dog Has Fleas" is what one sings to the four strings played open on one's uke.

Mixing up words of Formby classics at Dave's, in his music room, joined with the above silliness to make me write 'Leaning on a Window', still a staple of my live sets. Wholly to amuse Dave.

LEANING ON A WINDOW

I'm a fan of Formby, I get down on my knees
All my friends are plonkers and all their dogs have fleas
I can do the laugh (her-her) but I get in a fix
Because I get so nervous, the words all up I mix, so

I'm leaning on a window, when I'm cleaning lampposts
With a little Chinese laundry in my hand
If women like them like Blackpool rock

Only a Formby fan would understand
Why I'm leaning on a window, when I'm cleaning
  lampposts
With a little Chinese laundry in my hand

I went to the Society, my name was on the list
I had four drinks, one for each string and nerves did not
  exist
But I found out it doesn't help the mixed-up lyricist
To play the alcolele like a ukulelepist, so I'm still...

I met the Queen of Uke, I'd like to ukulay her
So smitten I fell on the floor, looked up her vuvuzela
With my little euphemism her ear has been abused
But when she takes a uke in hand, my words still get
  confused...

When I do Mr Wu, it's true, I'm a hoo-do, you-do man
In Auntie Maggie's nightshirt, I strum me fanlight fan
One thing that would just suit me, to turn out nice again
Is if everybody mixed it up – so please all join in,
  when I'm...

With a little Chinese laundry, proprietor George Formby
With a little Chinese laundry in my hand

One of my happiest memories of the time is when Dave
and I teamed up for a one-off gig doing country music, after

he was asked to play such material for someone's birthday do in a village hall in Suffolk. We discovered we both like old commercial 'cowboy' songs and old cowboy movies. So, we formed Hoarse Opera for one gig only, though we ended up doing two.

We had lots of fun rehearsing old numbers, finding old songbooks from his huge collection, mostly from boot sales and a few from mine. We both played guitars and ukes and I got a chance to even do a bit of lead on electric, a rare thing. I found it hard to stop doing fake cowboy talk. We ended with 'Twilight on the Trail', having seen off 'Ghost Riders' and 'Coming Round the Mountain'. The gig went well and we then did another one, a charity gig at Dave's local pub. I've still got the poster. Just fun and no ambition.

We also went to boot sales. Dave's style was so different here that, even if we went together, we wouldn't go around the stalls together. He was a 'get there early and whip round quick to find bargains' man, especially when it came to musical items. My mode is slow and late and ponderous. At Marks Tey, we would agree to meet at the good coffee stall, where proper coffees were available, at around 9.30am or 10am and compare purchases and sightings. We had mobile phones for any good thing we needed to consult on.

One day at Dovercourt, when they had monthly sales there, I found a brass instrument I couldn't identify. Dave was at home, so I phoned him and described it. "It's a tenor horn. Buy it if it's ten quid or less." It was and I did and later he played it on a recording I made. Dave had been in brass bands, as well as playing uke on TV, on a variety show where members of the Formby Society were guests, some years previously.

Dave's big boot sale claim to fame was finding a special old guitar. He phoned me one Sunday and told me I should come and look at a guitar he had got at Ardleigh, which had a sale on Sunday mornings close to where he lived. When I went over, he showed me a Clifford Essex Paragon, probably made in the 1930s. We found one online that had sold for two grand and were suitably excited. Only trouble was, Dave's £20 bargain had a huge screw through its heel, holding it together. We also discovered that Clifford Essex, a shop we both remembered from the 1960s near Leicester Square, still existed in name. Dave later phoned them and discovered it was run as an online banjo business by a chap called Clem Vickery. I immediately said, "My pal Cliff played drums with him in the Clem Vickery Velum Stompers!" We visited Clem, who remembered Cliff as "a lovely man" and we had a great, long chat. He got the guitar repaired for Dave.

Clem also ran a magazine, again with a taken-over name, BMG, standing for Banjo, Mandolin, Guitar. I wrote up Dave's guitar story for it and we took photos for the article. These were fun times.

With another couple of ukulele pals, Phil Manchester and Lance Rickman, we also formed Ukaholics Unanimous, who used to meet once a month to play uke songs. I remember Dave knocking us out with his version of his hero Louis

Armstrong's signature tune 'Sleepy Time Down South'. I liked it best when everyone did their party piece, rather than all playing together, as uke groups tend to do now.

At Dave's 70th birthday, his wife Sarah and I arranged for his favourite banjo uke player, the incomparable Andy Eastwood, to come and play. I sang a song for Dave, saying he was 'A Rare Old Man for a Song'. We both loved old expressions and he told me about a chap who kept buying bicycles in his village and how someone had described him as "a rare old man for a bike". Good old Dave. I really miss him. He really was a rare old man. Old in the sense of familiar, as he wasn't old in years and although I hadn't known him long, it always felt like we were old mates. Some friends are like you've known them always – new old friends. The immortal ukulele Dave, who was funny, intelligent, wise and talented. As Sarah had written on his gravestone, 'In Loving Memory of a Gentle Man.'

Let's start a band – Adrian's Bargain Bootsale Band – a supergroup formed for the purposes of this chapter. And let me introduce them, starting with the drummer, as they are at the back:

Buying a £10 tom this week was a prize in a scarce time for instruments. I had been amassing odd drums for some time. I'm no drummer, but I like to use bits of percussion for home recording. I nearly have a full kit of bits. The first thing I bought was an old pair of drum brushes. I played a cardboard box with these on a few early cassette recording overdubs. I think they came from a secondhand stall in Halstead market. My ambition at the time was to get a snare drum. I had little money in those days.

Colchester had a good antiques place with lots of stalls, much later and I bought a snare drum, part of an old Premier kit, for £30. I remember attaching it to my cycle's pannier rack with an elastic cord or two. I wonder if I had seen the drums, then returned the next day to try to get just one and thus taken the cords with me for the hopeful purpose. It seems likely. Later I bought cymbals and stands at various sales; sticks too. I found, years later, a bass drum that matched the snare, at Marks Tey. I wonder if they had been together when I could only afford one. The boot sale bass drum was only a tenner, but I got a pedal for it for a fiver a few weeks later. I still use them often. This year I've been hitting a small hand-tom and the bass drum with a stick and a sleigh-bell stick, to get a kind of Morris rhythm section. This sounds great to me. A 'Mr Bitsa' on percussion, really. Not too much clapping, it only encourages him.

Usually, the bass player comes next. You don't often see bass guitars at boot sales. My feeling is that people hang on to them. One stall holder showed me an old sixties Burns he had bought early at the sale once. Lovely, old and valuable too, but he didn't want to resell this bargain. You rarely see double basses either, not even the cases (see Weeks 6 and 7). Most of the bass guitars I've bought from shops, albeit often secondhand. If you have a bass guitar, you can usually get a gig, as there are few bassists to go round. My old Hohner headless bass, bought in the 1980s for £250, has held its value and earned its keep over the years, depping with folk dance bands and others. Even so, a couple of years ago I found a Fender bass bag for £7 at a boot sale, which I bought. Envious of Murray's lovely old Fender Precision and Jazz basses, I decided I needed a bass to go in it. Finding a Squire (cheaper Fender model) Jazz on Gumtree brought me from bag to bass-in-bag. The bass is made to look old, although it isn't really, but it plays great. I sometimes introduce Murray as Professor of bassology at the university of Groove.

I suppose keyboard players would be next. With this band it's accordion or harmonium. I think it was £20 I paid for an Indian harmonium, with some lovely drones. You pump the bellows with one hand and play with the other. It is a lovely thing and it worked fine, though now needs repair. I had seen Allen Ginsberg play one accompanying himself singing a song 'Broken Bone Blues' on TV once. It is an earlier version than the one he later recorded, more droney and poetic, just accompanied on his small Indian harmonium. Mine was a good boot-sale buy and worth loads more than the price paid.

I bought a Hohner Student accordion for £55 more recently and my friend John still has it, but I guess I have borrowing rights. I used this to record a slow, lost-love song. When I went wrong, I just started again from where I left off on a different track of the multi-track machine. Eventually I patched together a part, by deception really.

A few old melodeons have come from boot sales, but

usually they are instruments of limited lifespan. These button accordions often have cardboard bellows and they decay over time. Old Hohners are worth repairing if not too bad. But maybe eight years ago I did buy a good Pokerwork D/G Hohner for £50 that is in good order and worth at least six times the price paid, even second hand. I can still knock out a tune on it.

Do melodicas count? These are keyboard instruments and you can play chords on them. Not sure if Hohner still make them, but finding them is fun and they have a unique sound, so even pop musicians still use them for their tone. You'll hear them soloing over synths.

I do have a Yamaha keyboard bought for £15 in a junk shop. It has a sampling function and loads of strange sounds built in, and again is much sought after for its sounds and sampling. They go for £70 upwards now on the internet. But I'm not selling mine as I use it on my folk poetry projects for unusual noises. I'm delighted it's valuable. My cheap Casio from the same vintage, 1980s I think, is worth nothing but incomparable for cheap, cheesy noises, especially the tinny drums.

The lovely old LP case I bought this week is perfect for a melodeon. Not the card and thin plastic ones from the 1970s or 80s, but earlier, sturdier ones from earlier, sturdier decades. Cleaned and polished, lined with bubble wrap, they are funky looking for the casual box amateur. This one is a lovely deep blue.

Old Wheezy, on keys and buttons. Squeeze out a smatter

of appreciation.

There is such a thing as rock and roll excess but there is also rock and roll modesty. As we're approaching the frontline players, we have to remember the boot sale is full of the amateur and the semi-pro, the old pro and the hobbyist. I love a banjo myself and have one from a junk shop in Epping. When I realised he always priced them, of any make and condition, at £35, it was just a case of waiting till he got a decent one. I eventually found a nice Barnes and Mullins, quite playable. I used it in the Hooligan Band, a brilliant mixture of comedy and English folk dance, where I usually dressed in a dressing gown and pyjamas to play. We were led by a member of the Ukaholics, Phil Manchester. More recently someone offered me a zither banjo of good quality but needing some work for £10, as they didn't want to take it home from Marks Tey. My pal John Cubbin made a new nut and it is now playable and hangs around at home. I did see a few banjos this year but resisted asking the price, as I don't need another.

Banjo ukes, as above, you don't see often but they are around. There are some horrible, unplayable ones. There are banjo-mandolins, often with banana-shaped necks bent from the high tension of eight metal strings, though actually nice sounding if you find a good one. No-one famous plays one, so they don't sell, but I remember a busker playing music hall tunes on a banjo-mandolin, which sounded great.

Last year, I did what you were supposed to do if you deal instruments. I bought a good banjo uke for £25 and sold it for £50. It was a nice East German Musima model, which needed some strings and a bridge, which I had in stock. Probably worth more, even £100. My mate Nigel Burch of the Flea Pit Orchestra rarely uses any other make. A good Commie uke.

I am less sensible about wooden ukes and guitars and tend to let my interest overcome my modest sensibility. I have bought a few wooden ukes out of academic or over-enthusiastic reasoning, sometimes getting them playable, but then finding them not worth playing. Old ones are often not so great, especially now they are popular. I have been guilty of buying old guitars and any electric guitars out of pure enthusiasm and having something to get playable. The best ones are a 1960s Teisco Factory 'Raver', with that name on the headstock, worth a tiny bit more than it cost me to get working. My favourite is a cheap Stagg Telecaster copy, which sounded better than my actual Fender Telecaster bought new. It cost £15 and £40 to fix the electrics, but I do love it and use it. The 'Raver' I mean to sell one day but it looks good on the wall.

Trying to stop myself buying guitars I don't need can be difficult. A few years back, I bought a lovely old Martin 00018 from a dealer, where it was the cheapest guitar he had, at a couple of grand. As this cheaper one was as good as the others, though battered, I felt sympathy (or empathy) for this old crock and it came home with me. Unlike the rest of the guitars he had for sale, this one didn't come with a case. A couple of weeks later I spied at Horsley Cross an old blue/

grey hard case which looked to me of the same 1950s-ish vintage. I looked at its nice red interior and was not sure, but guessed it might just fit the Martin. I reluctantly paid £27, which seemed a lot for an old case, but my hunch paid off. It fits as if made for the battered Martin. I fettled the hinges and recovered a torn bit of the finish, with a small piece of cloth from under the lining. I cleaned it and touched up the gold clasps with a dab of paint, then polished the whole with silicone from a car cleaning can. This almost gave me as much pleasure as the lovely old guitar itself. It all seemed to fit, me and the guitar and the case.

New stuff now – I really don't like it in the main. I can't be scared that I might scratch its obscene shininess. The old, quality stuff is often better made and has matured. The Martin is the kind of thing I would have liked early on, if I could have afforded one. They were not so easy to find or afford before the internet, I have to admit.

There was a chap who used to come to the boot sales round here, but only for a couple of years. He used to have loads of guitars on show, but they were so overpriced, I don't think I ever saw him sell one. I think I only bought a dated guitar bag to fit the Raver and maybe an old strap from him. I timed these for when he was not himself present, as I guessed his wife would not ask so much for such small items. Even a plectrum he would overcharge for, so I bided my time. I always looked at his stuff and asked questions about it, though. His was more a museum mission I guessed, which was good so long as monetary value was never discussed.

There are some strange people in guitar and amp dealing, who like to boast of gigs and famous persons and fabulous deals. I do know someone who got an El Pico amp, as used by the early Beatles, at a local sale. There are lots of claims made about old Selmer amps, as the factory used to be in Braintree. I had a Selmer Little Giant (5 watts) myself, bought for £1 in Epping market, and I have a few old amps at home that I don't know what to do with. Or why I bought them. One I use for recording, which is a Peavey 45 watt with a spring reverb, but only a transistor one. It sounds good with tremolo through it, and it's loud. Again, I have had nice chats with overpriced vintage amp men, not mentioning money much. I am told the new ones are good, with modern hybrid valve sounds, but I'm not brave enough to try one, being mostly an acoustic guitar man.

Muso men can talk for ever about amps and guitars and I fall in with them easily, but only for a while. You do meet some nice old musos at boot sales, innocent men with innocent fantasies or even realities. Bless them all and tolerate their stories. Big hand for the old, battered model on guitar.

Singers often used to play harmonicas and I love a harmonica. Again, people are realising their value but finding a nice old Hohner 12-hole for £1 is still possible. I bought a full set of 10-hole copy-style vampers (all keys) for £8, a boxed set no less, which sound great. I always keep an eye out for a good harp. Often, they are knackered or cheap Chinese ones, but sometimes you still find one. None this year, however, though I saw some rusty overpriced ones. The blues and folk artists of the 1960s, me included, love a harmonica. 'Wheezy Anna' on the harp, which is a Leslie Sarony song title.

Singers need mic stands and mics. I love a stand, too, and music stands are common at boot sales. Ukulele Dave used to buy them all. I used to tease him that he had cornered the market in used music stands. I've bought a few too many myself and a few off him. He sold me a good case or two and I always look for old uke cases to do up. This year I did buy a desk mic stand that I'm using already (see Week 17). I'm the singer of boot sales here, obviously. Adrian May, boy soprano, as I sometimes say, when reduced to introducing myself.

Singers need recording, as I'm now doing. I use an old personal mini-disc recorder as a song notebook, bought for £5. These tend to be valuable with hobbyists now, so you don't see them so often. I had a lovely old Sony Pro Cassette machine which cost £250 new. Recently, it stopped working and disappeared into someone's workshop, who promised to try to find parts for repair, but never did. My good luck was to find one the same for £4 at a boot sale, where the seller had no idea this superior model was worth good money, even for parts. They seem to go for hundreds on the internet. I often pass by good recorders, like an old broadcast Uher I saw at Marks Tey. A lovely thing but I resisted for once.

Old muso talk, lost in equipment, doesn't make a band. You can bore people. But there's fun in the modest enthusiast and my friendship with ole Ukulele Dave was a bright spot in my life. A lovely man and kind and funny. I always imagine him around when I look at stuff today and long to tell him if I get something unusual, remembering our adventures in modest muso land. I remembering him laughing too much and nearly losing control of his car, as I played 'Where Did Robinson Crusoe Go, With Friday on Saturday Night?', newly arranged for the uke, in the passenger seat. I'd learnt it from two LPs: one bought for 50p by jazzman Clinton Ford and one more recently for £1 by Ian Whitcomb, author of *After the Ball*, a classic on popular music.

Let's end this gig with me and Dave laughing at a silly song, hoping that this ridiculous tale of isolation and the seeking of 'wild women' would add fun to the world, as it had for us.

Weeks 9 and 10:
FASHION

FRIDAY 25TH JUNE 2021. HORSLEY CROSS.

The Cosmic Doctrine. Dion Fortune. *50p.*

WEDNESDAY 30TH JUNE 2021. MARKS TEY

New floppy green cap. £12.

It had been a wettish month and it was raining gently again, though warm. The previous evening, in one of our long and wide-ranging phone calls, my friend Jo and I had been talking about Dion Fortune. These kinds of spooky connections seem normal to me anyway, but it was a good one to find her source book and only that the next day. This short visit to Horsley Cross was a strangely self-reflective one in more than one way. I was struck by a stall where I bought nothing but recognised everything. It was like a stall full of things I liked or sought: a Venus Pencils tin, not bought as I already have one that used to be my dad's. There were blank CDs, but I'd already bought and begged quite a few of them recently for music projects. I didn't need any more. There were guitar-type Jack leads, which I have loads of, and even a stop-watch – but a digital one. It was as if someone had cleared my house in a parallel universe. All was gently cosmic in the rain. I noted in my log, 'stall that is like it's yours'. That and *The Cosmic Doctrine*.

Dion Fortune I know little about, except this book and another one, from a charity shop, called *Applied Magic*. In that book I had found the entry for the shadow archetype (an unconscious aspect of the personality) really good. I was seeing my shadow that day. Both books were published in the 1980s by Aquarian Press, and this one was bought from an occult book shop in London. The 'Facing of the Shadow', as the author writes in a passage I had marked, implies the realisation of the reality of the subconscious mind and also the acceptance of material that is often at variance with the conscious mind. This seemed true on a wet Friday. The 'Dweller on the Threshold' is the sum-total of an individual's past lives, their own adverse character rising out into seemingly independent life. These two passages mix two archetypes of self-reflection, the Shadow and the Threshold Guardian. Both are manifestations of the self and its blockages. Threshold Guardians are usually seen as people you encounter in archetypal situations but must be, as she points out, also manifestations of self.

The Cosmic Doctrine I've read less of so far, as it seems to be her early mystic manifesto and, to my mind, is a bit less accessible. Her real name was Violet Firth and the strangely glam-rock penname feels a bit odd to my ears. It is something to do with 'God, not Fortune', which was a family motto. Mysticism was a hobby of posh people around the time of The Golden Dawn secret society in the late 19th and early 20th centuries, but I like the fact that Ms Fortune was later one of those mystics protecting England from invasion, when an army of occultists were trying to stop Hitler. This obviously worked, silly or not. They are a fascinating bunch and still deserve attention.

We cannot help wondering if this dabbling in the occult was just a hobby. But I have read enough of her and of W.B. Yeats, for example, to know that it meant everything to them. When I don't buy much, I can still find moments of self-reflection and on this day got plenty of it.

As I write, another source of self-reflection comes in the missing volume of *The Anatomy of Melancholy* by Robert

Burton (see Week 3). I had told Dave from the bookshop about my finding Volume One and buying Volume Two. He found me a Volume Three somewhere. Full melancholy! Again, more self-reflective reading.

Hats make you look at yourself. It was drizzly on the following Wednesday but a new hat stall appeared with a good salesman in charge of good new hats. He proffered a mirror and made you feel good, trying on a new hat. I had been looking for a bigger, floppier cap and I was delighted. I bought nothing else that day. Hats also add to your head in a cosmic way. They are like a penname, adding something to you. I have sometimes used the anagram 'Adam Rainy' for mine. I wrote something for students to read once, but didn't want them to feel constrained by the fact that I'd written it. One mystically inclined student girl divined it: only one in a few years of using the same piece. You try a penname on for size, for look.

Hats are reflective and attract jokes. I usually tell hat sellers, "I've got a big head," but as my dad used to say, "Never mind, son; there's nothing in it". This was an old line of my dad's but it still gets a laugh. I do have a big head. I remember another story of his about the old farm worker Jack Smith. My dad took him to Epping to buy a new cap. "What size?" asked the salesman in Pynes, the old departed department store. "Well, I've brought me head with me, ain't I?" responded Jack. A cosmic joke, somehow. Hats enhance the head.

I love hats but I didn't always get them. I think I was 23 when I did. At the time I was starting to lose hair from the front of my head. I didn't mind this. Nowadays, especially on screen, you rarely see a balding head. A bald man or a man in a hat is more self-reflective and honest than someone with a toupée or a hair transplant, which is rather false in its attempt at convention and conformism.

Hats were for old people but I'd always liked trying them on. My then girlfriend, Angela, used to say, "Give him a hat and a mirror and he'll keep himself amused for hours." I was in Notting Hill, of all places. Angela worked in London as a nanny and sometimes on Saturdays we went to the street market. I was overcome with the urge to buy a flat cap, like the old English folk-song guys used to wear. There was an old tailor's shop near the stalls and I got my first one. I have been a devotee of hats ever since. I soon wrote a song about it:

You may think I look a prat in me old flat hat
But me old flat hat is me pride and joy
You may think I look a twit but I am fond of it
Cause I'm only a country boy

I remember buying a new one a year or two later, when I took old Arthur, another of my dad's old countrymen pals, to Old Harlow. There was a shop exclusively selling clothes to older men. They had proper cord trousers, smart boots that looked like shoes, collarless shirts. A great and long-gone place.

I remember Arthur throwing his cap into the room from the door when he visited. "If it comes back out, you'll know you're not welcome," he said. I've done this a few times myself.

Every time I see a good hat, I buy it. I need a hat to protect me from the sun and the cold and the rain. Hats might seem showy to my own generation and I remember being mocked for wearing one, but people are more open-minded now, at least about appearance. A hat is a humble but significant thing, in that it gives a signal, a topping, even if not a 'fascinator'. I wrote an essay about titles for creative writers, where I said that titles are like hats. They tell you something significant, even the cosmic reaching of the mind upwards, as well as something utilitarian. They are honest and not a cause for self-consciousness. Unremarked wigs in men or lushly dyed hair of actors on TV are symptoms of horrible falsity. A hat is an honest attempt to bear the soul to heaven in a humble way.

I am pleased that now a hat is ignored. Poets and women who cycle like hats and I sometimes think that a hat means someone is a decent human. It seems to me that civilisation went wrong when the wearing of hats became outdated. When you see photos of old football matches and everyone is hatted, my heart lifts. It lifts like a hat in respect for a sane era. If I advertised for love, I would probably ask for 'a woman who might wear a hat preferred.'

Are you happy being ignored? As a teacher and folksinger,

I am used to it. Humility is a hat of honest need to be nearer God. When he was writing my favourite collection of his poems, *Pansies*, D.H. Lawrence used to wear a small African hat in bed, to keep his brain warm, I remember reading.

There is a pile of hats, old and new, mostly caps of one kind or another, in my hallway. I cannot resist a hat and like them as souvenirs. When I visited Tunisia, my pal Rachid heard me say I was sorry I hadn't had time to buy a hat, so he sent me a traditional *chechia*, a bit like a fez, with a tassel. Hats are traditional and innovations are slow to be accepted. Wearing a baseball cap in France in the 1990s, I was laughed at, as usually only young people wore them there, where such a cap was mostly disregarded back in England.

My dad always wore a hat and liked to wear one indoors at times. I have a patchwork highly coloured cap brought from a craft stall at Sidmouth Folk Week in Devon a few years ago and I sometimes wear it indoors. It gives me warmth, security, shields me from too much light and connects me with my dad. I could do with it now to shield my eyes from the winter sun. People wear party hats at Christmas and need to signal normal human excess in coloured paper. The humble cracker drives away the gloom of long nights. Hats celebrate our foolishness and need for reaching beyond.

As I write, this dark time of year, about the hats of drizzly June, we are contemplating further lockdowns due to the Covid pandemic. The time has become cosmic and dark again, like last year, last winter. My winter hat, bought in the first week, was worn often in the passing week. Now it is a bit warmer, my green floppy cap is best. The world closes towards Christmas and I am left alone with my hats, with my notions of what the world was in June and what it is now. Since retiring, I feel I am still trying to come to terms with what happened when the world also seemed to retire into restrictions.

Another cosmic happening was that, at the beginning of the first pandemic restrictions, a book fell off my shelves in the poetry section. This was a coverless version of Dante's *Purgatory*, bought for 20p. I started reading it. It felt like a guided vision of the times we were in. This is my version of Canto I:

A NEW PURGATORY
(after Dante, canto 1)

Hell is most popular
and you can see it from here -
wherever we are, we are in the middle of something

This suspension between worlds seems familiar
and inevitably allegorical –
denied some of it, we are struck by the beauty of the world

Unable to avoid the moral tone
and feeling we are being taught something –
we have to go down before we can go up

And re-ascend to the earthly paradise
we lately ruined –
we are in a place of humility and the purging of sins

There are layers to go through
in the little coracle of the self –
singing of that second realm no-one believes in

An old coverless book fell from the shelf
so I was bound to find it significant –
all places are earth; bound like purgatorio

I saw an old man solitary nearby
he said Who are you that against the dark tide
seek to flee the eternal prison?

You seek freedom which is precious
enough to give your life for –
so much is resonant now

First to wash away the taint
of the other place –
he plunged his hands into the spring dew

Second the reed used as a belt –
the self-renewing, fast-growing song
like the reeds near here where swans nest now

The reed that might vibrate the musical lift
and can be metaphor and poet
in a time when songs must form a blessing

I plucked the lowly plant
wherefore it did spring up again –
we pace a lowly plain, as if returning to a lost road

This still seems of now as I write, as if we are still struggling between states of safety and danger, suddenly aware of life's significances. This might have been time to write the whole of Dante's least-read epic, but I choose for now an epic of cosmic hats, which must be my blessing in this lonesome time, my hat against the storms and chills of heaven or hell. Hats are cosmic because they acknowledge the sky and the quick-growing reed that is both belt and song to hold us together as we return to a lost road. Could be a hatband.

Taking off a hat in respect is something the hatless are powerless to do. I take mine off when funeral processions pass. I go cap-in-hand into masked and respectful pharmacies and doctors' surgeries. A hat can be doffed and can act as a basket. My dad collected duck eggs in his hat when he was a farm worker in the war. He stirred them into his flask of coffee and quaffed the nourishing mixture when eggs were scarce.

Two more hats came from the same stall, as the new hat man was now there every week. One was a black one, similar to the green one and worn twice for funerals, so far. At the end of the season, I bought a lighter green one and had a long chat with the good hat man about the season.

Titles are hats and I like a title as well as a hat, as you can see from this harvest of text gathered against the winter dearth. I offer a cosmic hat of solstice and solitary goodwill as I raise a glass to absent friends from June to December.

"That which is above is like that which is below," is a statement associated with the Magician Hermes Trismegistus and seems to me true of hats, which reach, as we reach for them, for the metaphor above. Everyone has a hat, from the dunce to the archbishop, from the Magician to the Worker. The hermetic tradition is nothing to do with hermits but all have messages from the gods, via Hermes, the creative communicator, the original deliverer of messages, the mercurial. At Christmas my hermetic and Hermean hat confronts the taboo of being alone. Over the break, I'll be staying with my boot sale weeks, so my mind can wander in the still of winter to the green fields of the fair. I will see the hugeness of the world in the cosmic humility of hats.

Individualistic women hunt for unusual clothing at boot sales and I note them as I pass. I have often bought new T-shirts and this year some new spotted handkerchiefs. These I soaked in salt water to stop the dye running before washing. A good tip for cheap clothes, which youngsters don't seem to know these days. There is a cheap stall for branded jeans at Marks Tey. When my last but one leather jacket wore out, which had cost a hundred or more, I got one from a boot sale, costing only £10, which lasted years. This one is still good, but has been surpassed by a posh one for a couple of hundred, from which the buttons fell off. So, apart from shoes, I could be entirely dressed in boot sale garb. If you buy new clothes at boot sales, you need to look in the packaging, get it out of the bag, to make sure it's good and the right size.

The other thing I bought once was when I got fed up with departmental meetings at work. A shell suit seemed a good idea. A fake branded one for about £12 fitted fine and I still have it; black with red piping. I might start wearing it to write in, as it is warm and comfortable and reminds me of my desire to confront their bourgeois cheese-pairing with a bit of my old working-man's rough style. A cap would have set it off anomalously but well.

I raise my hat and think of new hats, new titles, new writing like new outfits tried on. I throw my hat in the air; as above, so below, all signalled in the hat that raises. Hermes is usually depicted with winged heels but also with a broad brimmed cap. A modern depiction of this messenger of the gods, giving the gift of self-reflection might be a helicopter hat, a hat with a revolving light on it or a hat with a ponytail attached, signifying movement. He does the head and feet, the movement of the self from its stuckness in the everyday. The hat that elevates. Getting a hat is half way to winged sandals.

As Oscar Wilde didn't say
  we're all in the shit
But those wearing hats, imaginatively
  are half way out of it

As Dion Fortune notes in her introduction to *The Cosmic Doctrine*, when a work is vast in concept, it is necessary to resort to the extensive use of metaphor. And metaphor, she says, is an endeavour to convey abstract ideas in reasonably concrete form. The big metaphor is the highest hat which expands the mind for all writing, I reckon.

Week 11: SMALLNESS

FRIDAY 2ND JULY 2021. HORSLEY CROSS.

3 tins Heinz tomato soup. £1.

2 packets Hobnobs. £1.

Ancient Monuments: East Anglia.

The Village Labourer Volume II.

Local History for Beginners.

The Dairy of a Farmer's Wife. 4 books for 80p.

Dictionary of Saints. John J. Delaney.

The Second Book of Irish Myths and Legends. Eoin Neeson.

A Celtic Miscellany. 3 books for £1.

The East Anglian magazine. 50p.

The Oxford Companion to Local History. 50p.

Ideal hardback notebook. £1.

New potatoes. £1.

FRIDAY 9TH JULY. HORSLEY CROSS.

Donald McGill Card, 'Little Winkle'. £1.36.

3 spotted hankies. £1.

Teach Yourself Non-Fiction. 30p.

Colchester Past. 50p.

Bayeaux Tapestry. King Penguin. £1.

100 Poems. Ella Wheeler Wilcox. Mini-book. 30p.

Local material of historical interest provides some great sources for writing as well as for deepening your roots to the place you live. This was ingrained in me, I think from my father, who on moving to the countryside just before the Second World War, had become an agricultural journalist. Turning back to the land was to become a theme post-war, as it had been after the first one. In times of crisis, people look for depth, instinctively rebalancing the world. There are stories everywhere and it feels like a duty to let them echo through your world. Boot sales are a good source for this kind of folk literature.

People like local stuff, despite the cultural imperatives of the media and of publishing. I consider it a scandal that in Essex the university and the local council have rarely undertaken any local publishing, with a few exceptions. BBC local radio has similarly neglected its own brief to the point where their bland output has been centralised to computer-generated playlists. They are a disgrace, especially when they started so well and have declined so steeply. When I did something on local radio, they actually seemed ashamed of themselves.

Colchester has the local studies library for Essex in its central library. They used to have specialist local historians working as staff, who would help you find materials. I used to take my MA students there and someone would talk to them about the wealth of material they have. These wonderful resources are on the decline and under threat from central government, who only count money. These quiet archives are actually our life-blood.

In my recent book *Tradition in Creative Writing*, I wrote extensively about a locally discovered apple, the Discovery. In a small pamphlet on its home village, I was able to find the address for the 'Mother Tree' and visit and photograph it. This information was not available on the internet. These kinds of research gems seem of such vital importance to me, for many reasons.

The world can still function at a more local level and indeed it always must do, despite material considerations of the big world of money, who want us all to be homogenised consumers. When I told the chap who ran The Minories gallery, in Colchester, that our duo event, featuring poems and songs about local hero John Ball and about the local vicar who championed him, Brian Bird, would sell out, his look told me he thought me arrogant. I was then able to reassure him that anything with a local history connection would do well. I wasn't wrong. The room was packed. Writing on local subjects is a good way for writers to start a career. And I would say also a good way to continue, to have continuity.

The first sunny Friday of this long week found me lots of local historical stuff and some of the best of it went to my friend Elaine Barker, who writes about Peldon and adjoining local villages, there on the way to Mersea. She writes a column for the parish magazine.

The East Anglian magazine, from the 1950s and 60s, is always good, especially if there's a particular item of interest. With this one, from August 1957, it was an interview with Alfred Munnings, the second most famous artist from

Dedham, the first being John Constable. Earlier (see Week 3) I had bought a book club edit, three-into-one volume of Munnings' autobiography, and I have been fascinated by this brilliant and often overlooked artist for some years now. In the interview, in old age, he sounds grumpy but still game.

The Munnings' Museum is a lovely place to visit. His art is wide-ranging and full of energy and they only have wall-room to display a small proportion of it. His studio in the garden is as he left it and large and complete. The tea room is a separate building and a really good, airy place. The whole of the grounds are lovely too. It has a relaxed and homely feel and great, friendly staff.

I used to tell my students how I had got into discussion there with a female volunteer, probably about Munnings' local sensibility and closeness to the people around him. This deep chat then carried on when the house was closed. We stood outside in earnest discussion. Suddenly she looked down, and then exclaimed, "We're standing in a fairy ring!" I had already noticed this. Fairy rings are wanderings, their fungal growth quite natural and supernatural at once, somehow, as local art and writing can be. She looked at me with blazing eyes.

My story would lead up to this moment, then stop. I was demonstrating creating mythic atmosphere. They would want to know what happened next. "Did you go back to her place?" a male student asks, hopefully, wistfully. "Nah, I just got in me car and went home," I said, which was true.

I recently bought another *East Anglian*, dated December

1961, as it has a lovely Christmas cover of a snowy church. I've photocopied this onto a few cards but also given the magazine to Elaine, mentioned above, for Christmas. This one came from Dave's bookshop in Stoke-by-Nayland. These things we have in common are the most valuable.

Munnings trained on the job as a commercial artist in Norwich, not in art school, and has the energy and naivety of a local artist with a national profile. He painted lots of horses but lots of other stuff too. He retained the air of the autodidact, which I like and like to think I still have. The local artist retains their small scale as a guard against pomposity and assumed superiority. To the BBC, 'local' is a dirty word, so they say "the news where you are". I am a regional variation, determinedly provincial. But then so was Thomas Hardy, so was D.H. Lawrence. Shakespeare resorted to the Forest of Arden himself and returned home after London.

Amid the books on local history, you might notice, above, an Irish interlude. The most interesting of these is *The Second Book of Irish Myths and Legends*. The others seem to tell a story of someone living in Essex with Irish roots. Like many English, there are many connections here with Ireland. My branch of the May family were, a few generations back, Irish immigrants, for example. Braintree in the 1970s had many Irish families living there and a bunch of covert police checking for IRA sympathies, I happen to know, from friends on all sides.

These three books, which might have belonged to someone called O'Reilly, as that name is in the *Legends* one, tell a story of roots seeking, just as one might do through local history. The Penguin anthology *A Celtic Miscellany* is one I already have and I even translated, sort of, a poem from it, called 'Who Will Buy a Poem?' To which my answer was 'Fuckin' no-one – that's who!' This poem regrets the current times when poetry is not respected. It seeks the old poetic past, the old poetic roots, just like me here.

The *Dictionary of Saints* is very much a Catholic book, with no Saint Adrians in it. I went seeking a Saint Adrian in Scotland once, but that's another story. The *Legends* book has weight for me, as it was actually published in Cork in 1966. It looks like a kids' book, but the scholarly introduction tells you otherwise. I have been reading the last tale in the book, 'The Sickbed of Cuchulain'. This hero appears in several sections of the *Miscellany* also. His name is spelt in several different ways and there is plenty about him available online. Two things caught my attention. I have written about what I call Aviantrophy (birds into human, humans into birds, with the supernatural involved) and although this does not appear so directly, it is folly and vanity in relation to the magic of birds that undoes the hero, which leads to his sickness and death. He is exiled from life and undone by magic.

Violence and magic seem to dominate his stories. He is the hero of unbridled anger, whose blood boils in battle. Yet he is undone by magic. Apparently both sides in northern Ireland claimed him as theirs. Despite great power, he is the model of suppression, which is the suppression of a people, as we have sleeping sickness and are unable to wake up to the balance of our own inner strength. He needs anger management but also magic management. Might he turn magic to positive use? Might his sleep turn dream into prophecy, in Dudley Young's resonant phrase? Lady Gregory, associated with Yeats, wrote about Cuchulain's myths, too, so there are many magical and local connections.

In the tale, he catches little birds for women. Then he sees more birds, but these are not ordinary. He catches two glorious birds, more beautiful than any of the others, that are linked together by a chain of red gold. As the birds come to him, slowly and majestically, they make soft, sweet music that lulls all that hear it to sleep. These godlike birds are obviously not mere birds. He tries nonetheless to bring them down in vain and they disappear. This is the start of his sickness and death. He cannot manage the magic. He goes into suppression, into unbalance. Must he retell his own myth to reconnect his action and his magic?

This book was published when Ireland had gained its magic again, or so it seemed. I have often felt the truth of the fact that the British suppressed themselves first, before the rest of the empire. In our long decline, in our little local histories, we sleeping heroes are trying to rebalance the anger and the magic ourselves. The English now sleep, still looking for our myths to help us respect the godlike qualities of the magic song of the reunited twin birds linked together with a chain of red gold, making soft, sweet music.

In the few times I have visited Ireland, I found it amazingly home-like and the magic seemed respected in a way us English can only envy, wedded to our decline. They are older than us in this reclaimed respect for their own culture and younger than us as a nation grappling with its freedom in the main. In our potential independence, I feel an affinity which is mythic, peaceful and balanced between us. I remember lovely Irish storyteller Packie Byrne, who visited folk festivals in the 1980s and what a laugh we had together. I remember Rosie Stewart, from the north, whose singing and whole attitude made me want to take up smoking, drinking and fighting. Once, at a festival, a bit drunk, I said to her as she passed, "I love yer, Rosie!" She glanced at me and said, "I love you too, darling," as she went on her way, as if it was the most natural thing in the world – which it is of course.

This Irish interlude brings me back home again to my local studies with renewed interest. I have happy memories of my 50th birthday in Cork, where the Legends book was published. It is the littleness of England I like, 'little' being a common word in English, especially in northern humour. My little Winkle card is a collectable Donald McGill, again from the 1960s, and has the old song lyric on it. "I can't get my winkle out / Isn't it a sin? / The more I try to get it out / The further it goes in!" Littleness and innuendo are English traits, our sleeping in spite of magic, or its antidote.

I was pleased to find one mini-book this year, which I only

buy when they are cheap enough, as they are collected and can be valuable. I have a small collection of mini-books – under ten. If you want an exact definition, you can look elsewhere, but I mean books of roughly 3" by 2" and a few variations. Anything pocket-sized is nice.

100 Poems by Ella Wheeler Wilcox is one of The Miniature Series published by Nimmo, Hay and Mitchell Ltd, undated, given by 'Bob' in 1921. I like the Hay and Mitchell bit, as it looks like May and Mitchell, the song-writing duo's name for a group I was in, Spring Chickens. Its 160 pages are neatly printed and it is a lovely little object. These days I need a magnifying glass to read it. For 30p it is irresistible, really.

Ella herself is interesting. She was unfortunate enough to be popular and accessible in her own time, so is now overlooked and laughed at, especially as her work has a kind of piety unfashionable these days. Each age has its own kind of piety and her late Victorian or Edwardian US sensibility has long been the least fashionable with the literati. But she has cool aspects, for me. She wrote memorable stuff and was a mystic, into theosophy. She wrote several poems that have commonly known phrases: "Laugh and the world laughs with you," for one small sample. She has featured among the mocked and will easily be found in the materials for Week 15: Bad Poetry, in this book.

"How does love speak?" she asks in the first poem. "In the proud spirit suddenly grown week – The haughty heart grown humble..." You get the idea, but I like this kind of stuff you read in neglected books at sales. She is lyrical and has skill and her stuff sticks. Her 'Voice of the Voiceless' poem is for animal rights and she deserves attention from those less snobbish. I like someone who could call a book *Poems of Passion*.

Mini-books tend to have nice end papers. A black, modern one, bought maybe last year, is called *Get Published in Six Months or Less*, by Scott Edelstein, and again has US connections, being published in the States. It is actually quite good and offers advice about writing locally as a way in, something I have advocated myself in this book. Local, small publishers are good to look out for, in terms of interesting reading and research and current ones for getting published. Publishing doesn't always have to mean big business. Sometimes it's good to keep it small.

Mini-books are often leather-bound. I have *The Story of Shakespeare*, *Flowers of St Francis* and *Great Thoughts from The Ancients*; also *Poems of Christina Rossetti*, again by Nimmo, in a lovely red suede. *Poems by Matthew Arnold*, also by Nimmo, is in a larger 3½" by 4" size. There is a list of their miniature books in the back of this one. The Rossetti seems to be in the Ruby Series, in calf-skin, and is a bit collectable.

The oldest one I have is the first I got, I think, as a gift from my dad. *The Singer's Companion and Carnival Friend* is probably from the 1830s and has some lovely illustrations of the cartoonish variety. It is 250 pages long and even has an index. The words to the song 'Cheery Ripe' are in it and

I need to pay it the respect Dad suggested in 1986, on my 36th birthday. It consists of songs from theatre shows in the main.

Last Poems by Housman is a bit too big, but I keep it with the small, as it seems to belong. It seems to me you have to be big to make it into a miniature book and I aspire to such minimalism myself, to such humility. That is how love speaks, as Ella says.

The other things bought are food, sometimes locally produced, and Horsley Cross is a smaller place and seems to offer comfort sometimes missing in the grander Marks Tey fairs, however much I love them. The humble pursuit of roots seems to gather up my potatoes, my mini-book, my local and Irish root-seeking, as does the small Ideal notebook and the need to write good non-fiction. I imagined I had little to say here, but the small contains the larger theme, as a world in a grain of sand.

I haven't had a chance to mention J.L. Carr's 4" by 5" poetry series from the 1970s, but I have yet to find one at a boot sale. I have one of Blake, bought new in 1973 and one on the Peasants' Revolt, bought on the internet. Something to look out closely for next year.

I often find pocket-sized books in the Canterbury Poets series, published by Walter Scott, edited by another poet, William Sharp (Fiona McCloud) around the turn of the 19th into 20th centuries. I have a handful of these and find them hard to resist. One called *Fairy Music* has an introduction and is edited by A.E. Waite, of the Golden Dawn and tarot card fame. Again, these are collectable. In my book *The Magic of Writing* (2018) I wrote a poem, beginning, "Books about fairies should be small / And seem to say almost nothing at all." Phil Terry (see Week 13) has a small book just out with the Red Ceilings Press, who do poetry.

While writing, I remember that Allen Ginsberg's books were published in the Pocket Poets series by City Lights Books. I remember buying these as a teenager, in Better Books, off Charing Cross Road.

The tiny ring binder I bought at the end of the year counts too (see Week 20). My friend Dr Kate Dunton, of the Sainsbury Centre gallery at UEA in Norwich, once visited me and pointed out that I have many miniature things about my place. I knew this, but hadn't noticed in the way she had. We assembled some, including mini-books, like an art assemblage. I think she took some photos.

Again, I notice my collection of Canongate Pocket Canon series of individual books from *The Bible*, each introduced by a known writer. My copy of Ecclesiastes in this series became my constant companion, with its introduction by Doris Lessing, when I was writing my poetic commentary on the Book, called *Preacher: The Vanity Games*. I wish Canongate would publish these poems in a similar 6" by 4" edition. Maybe I am too humble for a small book.

My final small-scale idea here is for a book that mimics the size and shape of a smart phone. You could replace your phone with it. You could choose your own selection, so it was as commonplace as your phone. It could call attention to its humility, locality and particularly by being called *Find Yourself Within.*

LAYTON & JOHNSTONE

TIME

THE LONESOME SOUND OF HANK WILLIAMS

mono

The Lonesome Sound
of

HANK
WILLIAMS

The best of
John D. Loudermilk

Week 12: HANK

WEDNESDAY 14TH JULY 2021. MARKS TEY.

The Legendary Hank Williams. 6 LP boxed set. £2.

Lefty Frizzell CD. 50p.

New hat, black, floppy cap. £9.

Selected Poems. Alison Brackenbury. 50p.

2 Lonnie Donegan CDs.

Time (The Revelator). Gillian Welch. CD.

Carson Robinson CD. 3 for £4.

Self-Instructor for English Concertina (1858). £1.

What is it about Hank Williams? For me, he is a resource, a source of comfort and inspiration when all else seems shallow or sickening. I know others feel the same about him. Many US songwriters have written songs about him. He is a myth of suffering, the master of melancholy, even an anatomist of melancholy and sincerity. Part of it must be in his voice, so full of feeling and so open and expressive. 'Cold, Cold Heart' comes on the first of the LPs and you know he is poet and singer unsurpassed. My friend Pete Booth called him "the Keats of the 20th century" and I think there's something in it, rather than "the hillbilly Shakespeare". It is the intensity of the voice, first and most reachingly, in that he reaches out like few can. Like Roy Orbison said of the other singers in The Traveling Wilburys, "I am a singer – these guys are vocal stylists." Hank is the singer and the rest of us are mere stylists, or not even that.

I am playing this boxed set of 6 LPs as I write, which I never would do normally, preferring silence, or traffic and nature, for writing. This first one is called *Hits*. World Records was a club you joined and provided access to serious listeners in the form of boxed sets. I could never afford to join when young, but I have bought quite a few of their music hall albums over the years on that exclusive label, as well as country. This set was from a relatively young chap selling off his country collection cheap. There are loads of Hank CDs out there, for not much money, and I already have most of the songs here on LP or CD, but I couldn't resist the set. This year, I'm a sucker for boxed sets of all kinds. But an excuse to write about Hank must also have been in my mind. I had a lovely long chat with the young country fan, telling him about the Ken Burns documentary about the history of country music and sharing enthusiasms.

The songs on this side are mostly very familiar and often tending to the upbeat. Those are fine and provide contrast but it is the sheer melancholy we seek in his voice, I am convinced. I think this is also true of Bob Dylan and other great popular music of all kinds. The Anatomists of Melancholy might not be a great name for a band, but it is the band all good singers are in, I reckon. Side two promises more melancholy and, in real time, I am about to get to it.

It probably helps that Hank seemed to find really good players for his band. They emphasize the beat, at his insistence, I've read. His fiddle players and steel players are all great and you hardly notice there are no drums.

'I'm So Lonesome I Could Cry' is rhythmic here, and modern interpreters are tempted to slow it down, but Hank intones over a waltz that sounds even brisker than I remembered. The words and tone of voice are again highlighted. There is nothing in pretending to melancholy by slowness or pathos. This most unselfconsciously pathetic song thus transcends itself because it is done with a kind of formal melancholy country allows. Hank was not exceptional in the forms he used. They were the usual, even conventional musical clothes of his genre. On the surface his records sound like others from his era. It is his writing and vocal performance that make him exceptional. It is not entirely innocent and naïve either. He is a consummate and even effortless writer and performer. Naturalness is not unskilled in many ways. It must be achieved and maintained.

The Lefty Frizzell CD proves this, as he is a good contemporary but, subtly, just not in Hank's class, though worthy of attention as a songwriter of note. Dylan recently referenced his title 'Rough and Rowdy Ways' for example.

'My Heart Would Know' is not a song I know well. It feels upbeat again but its ruthless simplicity is artful beyond any patronising idea of country dumbness. It is heart knowledge, heart skill that tells beyond the lips of other singers.

This time of year, at the time of writing, seems right to revisit the summer of investment in an excuse to listen to Hank. It is in between Christmas and New Year and a lonely and quiet day. I've moved a laptop to the living room, which is warmer and where the record deck rests. It is no time for 'half-hearted love', but for finding the consolations of expressed melancholy. Hank can do resigned like no-one, so 'Why Should We Try Any More?'. Hank was not an innovator, he was conventional, but the convention allowed for, or he made it fit for, his genius to write and sing through. His greatness is undiminished and gets better the more you hear it.

The second LP is labelled *Country Favourites* and is Hank as cover artist. They are all good, of course, but lack a bit of the focus of his own material. Bob Nolan of the Sons of the Pioneers is featured as a writer, another essential one from the era; as soulful and another invisible influence. Fred Rose is also featured as a writer here, and he was Hank's mentor, being his publisher, producer and general encourager, early on. There are some rarities here and for a fan like me, its lovely to hear Hank learning his trade. Fred Rose was a shameless poet of the tearful and broken-hearted. 'No One Will Ever Know' is a model of male repression expressed. On this first side there is even the song that Hank made so much his own that it is assumed he wrote it – 'Take These Chains from My Heart.' 'Pale Horse and His Rider' is apocalyptic in title but again you feel Hank was learning it rather than singing it here.

I even like corny songs like 'Wedding Bells'. You have to suspend your disbelief to like country music at times, though Hank at his best transcends this. He was my route into appreciating what seemed very unfashionable to my 1960s ears. Later, in the 80s, I gave cassette copies of the *40 Greatest Hits* double LP, bought in the 70s, to band-mates, to effect their transformation.

Leon Payne was the songwriter Hank seemed to be most comfortable with, being a great poet of melancholy like Hank. 'They'll Never Take Her Love from Me' is here on this disc but not 'Lost Highway', beloved of Dylan and other songwriters for its resonant evocation of life on the road, with the road as a big metaphor. That song is on a later one of the discs, I am pleased to notice. There are a few here with unforgivable added-later strings and other such insulting, sweetening nonsense. Hank's education in the apocalyptic is here again in 'The Battle of Armageddon', though it is not a great song in itself. Is this working? Listening to Hank? If so, I can stand it. 'Please Don't Let Me Love You' ends the LP and he makes it his own, in tone and appreciation of the words as he delivers them so expertly.

The third disc is titled *Lonesome and Blue* and they got his subject right, unashamedly so. There are a few unfamiliar songs here I'm looking forward to. The tone is mostly serious in country music, but the Carson Robison CD shows a neglected side of humour in the old cowboy themes, which is still neglected. I love Robison's drollery and I have 78s by him which are funny with the dark humour of the poor. Even Hank tried a comic song or two early on, and humour is always there in his up-tempo stuff. Singers do comic material early on, then get to take themselves too seriously later on. I must get back to the sad and the comic, as these are closest to real life and less self-important. Carson Robison's band were the Pioneers, hence the Sons of the Pioneers. Pioneers' Grandsons, anyone?

Very glad that 'Low Down Blues' is on this side, as it was the model for Warren Zevon's 'Your Shit's Fucked Up', a favourite of mine. There's a great solo performance of this on the internet, from the *Later... with Jools Holland* TV show. For once I see the point of a big collection, as there are some good songs here which must be rare, like 'The Blues Come Around'. I didn't need this set, and may have even only bought it because I might write about it, but I'm pleased with the third disc. The sleeve notes here are good on his early life's sadness.

Last night on TV there was an evening devoted to Steven Sondheim, which seemed very showbiz to me, and Hank is the antidote to all that unresolved complication that Sondheim's songs exhibit. And I like Sondheim in the main. In his sadness and tragicomedy, Hank is resolved, as if a song is a play in itself. I am less likely to give up showbiz today – the world's indifference makes no difference to me. There's no one like Sondheim really but plenty like Hank. Originality is the thing in overdeveloped artforms, but in the popular arts it is a cultural environment that lets a genius emerge. Sondheim seems worked at, where Hank has worked to be natural.

The Beatles were not unique but all the bands, or groups, and there were many, in Liverpool, allowed them to be better. Hank is like this and his genius is organic, not to say he didn't work hard on it. You get the feeling Hank was never self-important. He had a shoebox full of lyrics, they say, and was always writing. You can't imagine Hank teaching his own work to over-serious young men.

On side two there is a very traditional folk-sounding minor key song, a rare thing for Hank. 'Alone and Forsaken' is a new one for me and would sound good unaccompanied. I make a mental note.

Disc four is titled *Songs of Faith*, which must mostly come from his religious persona Luke the Drifter, not mentioned here, even in the sleeve notes. And his most famous religious song, 'I Saw the Light' is not here, strangely, anywhere on the six LPs. This reminds me that Lonnie Donegan recorded a gospel album, which I have. The huge haul of five CDs of Lonnie, in two volumes, bought this week, does not have my favourite, his version of 'His Eye is On the Sparrow' on them. But I loved the English gospel flavour of this and did my own version in our skiffle and revolt show, *The Ballad of Brian Bird and John Ball*. There does seem to be a bit of barrel scraping here on side one. The sleeve notes again mention an interview with Hank's mother, where she says he put his whole heart into singing, to which the writer adds his whole intelligence. Spot on, Mum.

Old country songs do not shrink from death, which is again reassuring. I'm looking forward to side two, at least it has 'The Angel of Death', one of my favourite obscure Hank songs which I do have elsewhere. Religion is a relief, as it should be, facing sin and death with open hands. Like Hank, religion is not afraid of simplicity and must always return to it. The other version of 'The Angel of Death' I have is better, but it is still a great song, mesmerising in its directness.

Disc five has the incomparable 'Lost Highway' on side one and Leon Payne's song shows Hank's rootedness in his musical world. This fits the title of the disc – *Folk Ballads*. Most songs here are not narrative, as ballad implies, but they are generally archetypal, as Hank was drawn to the classic themes of song. There are also some Luke the Drifter songs here, which are religious in tone. Hank's traditionalism took for granted its universal themes, its Biblical roots and its moral tone. Are these things unavailable to us now? I don't think they are. I think we have to re-simplify ourselves as writers, to remind people of the clarities of the past.

If you listen to the radio, my guess is that at least 60 per cent of songs, including those from Radio 3, have mostly or partly inaudible lyrics. The thing with early country music is that the lyrics are to the front and clear as a bell. You don't bury Hank in the mix. Why would you? I'm such a stickler for this that when a friend of mine's son was recording with his band, I sent the expected message, not having heard a bar of any of the songs. 'Adrian says turn the vocals up,' I heard his Dad say. I was out in the garden. I heard a chuckle from the son. Clarity and simplicity threaten the mire of complexity the modern world relies on, with its machines and literalism and offence to be taken. Hank's Luke character was an attempt to be more simple and honest, even moral. It often falls into mawkishness but the attempt is instructive.

Hank refreshes us when we are overwhelmed with the complications of the world and of artists who feel they have to strangle their own voices. The last track on side one is his mentor Fred Rose's lovely 'Waltz of the Wind'. Plaintive was Rose's best mode. This and 'Ramblin' Man', along with 'Lost Highway' are prize enough on this first side.

Another orchestral mistake swamps the version of 'Lonesome Whistle' on side two, where the vocal sounds pushed to the back and tinny. "Just a kid acting smart / I went and broke my darling's heart...." I shudder to hear the backing imposed.

Hank did not really do narrative songs and the one attempt

here, a version of 'The Banks of Ponchatrain', is not a success. His songs are more essays in mood and communication of hurt and defeat. Ballads, but not in the literary sense. 'I'll Be a Batchelor 'til I Die' is worth the listen and has a comic edge, again in the tradition of single men's songs, like 'Little Sod Shanty' by the Carter Family. 'Wearin' Out Your Walkin' Shoes' is programmed intelligently: "You can't live with 'em, you can't live without 'em…"

I wonder if anyone else listened all through to these discs. They sound unplayed and they have no dust on them. I'm on my last one and I've loved it, even the bad or indifferent stuff. Hanging out with Hank is curative. He recorded lots of songs in his short life. This boxed set is from 1978, just before digital technology was to take over and, for all its shortcomings, Hank shines through. Hank Williams sings Hank Williams seems excessively obvious, as he always did, in the main. Ninety-six songs is quite a big bunch of them, but it's been no problem. He's one of the few I can bear in any mood, never less than bracing and inspiring too. While writing this I thought of a failed attempt at a song I made called 'Vow of Simplicity'. It begins, "If you've read Hank Williams, if you've heard William Blake…" perhaps too cleverly and paradoxically, equating the two prophets of simplicity. "It opens you to visions, it opens you to pain / It opens you to mockery / If you've taken a vow of simplicity." Maybe it was too complicated. Simple things are hardest to understand. And to write.

The last side I'm pleased to note starts with 'My Love for

You' – which continues "has turned to hate'. Here Hank is fearless again, even shocking. Directness has its place still and I can't think of a recent writer who would be so bold, really, as they hedge round their adolescent fantasies with inaudible verbiage. Again, I have a better, starker recording of this song elsewhere, as this one feels dubbed over, sadly. More barrel scraping, more crappy orchestral stuff and even naff backing vocals, but I don't mind. I know most of the songs by heart, from repeated listenings in the car, after my own gigs. It was my custom to listen to Hank on my way home and gently harmonise to myself. He is someone that understood and the understanding of the human condition transcends time and space.

The last side ends with two songs I don't know, like a treat. 'My Sweet Love Ain't Around' is a sad, rhythmic good one, while 'Fool About You' is kind of rock and roll and even features a more rock-sounding guitar. Not a classic but a short, unusual ending: "I'm gonna get gone."

In 2023, it will be 100 years since Hank's birth and 70 years since he died. Yet no definitive collection of his recordings exists, because, a website devoted to him says, of contractual difficulties. Your best bet is the *40 Greatest Hits* set. But anything is good, as it tends to come cheap and is always unfailingly inspiring.

The album I've listened to most from this week of buying is Gillian Welch's *Time (The Revelator)*, which has Hank Williams' apocalyptic feel to its title track and themes. It is a melancholy masterpiece. The track I've played repeatedly is the gloomy 'Everything is Free' about the decline of the record industry, which is where I've felt I've been hanging out as I listened to 12 sides of Hank. "I could get a straight job / I've done it before / I don't mind the working hard / It's who you're working for," she laments. The whole tone of the CD is minor and elegiac, with even a song about Elvis's death. The long closing song is a lamenting 'I Dream a Highway', like the lost highway of Leon Payne and, at nearly 15 minutes, a sad turning away from the myth as much as a running towards it. But she and her partner David Rawlings have the simplicity down still and prophetically. In this 2001 album they are Hank Williams' true inheritors somehow, direct where others pose, and unashamed in their darkness.

I've not really listened much yet to the Lonnie stuff, but he had a directness too. His comic songs show he was not shy of being true to himself. The man on the stall where I bought the CDs this week said his dad, retired to Spain, met Lonnie, who had done the same. They got on pretty well. I remember Lonnie reputedly asking for a cup of tea when a minder at a festival was anxious at his lack of 'rider' demands. Was Lonnie a bit of a Hank? No, but his voice has a directness and skiffle was a good attempt at a vow of simplicity. I could have a week with Lonnie soon.

My dear, late friend Mick Graves, a lovely singer and fiddle player, recorded a version of this old song of mine, below, which is another attempt to get near Hank. He inspires, but we rarely live up to him. I wonder how many songs have been written about him? As many as about Dylan? There are about 100 recordings of songs about Hank. Here's one attempt of mine from a few years' back. My new hat this week was a black one, for funerals, incidentally, for more positive melancholy.

HANK WAS NO SAINT (AND I AIN'T)

Some folks get famous for drinking
Some for just living so clean
Whatever they do's superhuman
That's what their publicists mean
Whatever image I go for
I'll still be a fool if I boast
But even Hank Williams was human
And I am more human than most

Hank was no Saint, and I ain't
What you get is less than you see
Hank was no Saint, and I ain't
So keep expecting the worst from me

I'd swear my love like the next man
If I was the man next to you
I've got the best of intentions
Though ones I've fulfilled are so few

And I can't stop myself thinking
When of my strong feelings I speak
How many times in the morning
The strong stuff has made me feel weak

Some people like to make icons
Out of their favourite star
But they soon find out that people
Are people whoever they are
Then with their scandalised faces
They cause the icon to act hurt
They should say I con myself now
When they throw all that stardust and dirt

Maybe I've heard too much lying
Seen all that pie in the sky
Maybe a part of me's dying
If that must be so, let it die
If I am fooling you darling
I'm fooling myself the same way
So please don't you think too much of me
You'll avoid disappointment that way

Week 13:
THE CONCRETE PAST

WEDNESDAY 21ST JULY 2021, MARKS TEY.

Stainer Model, German violin. £30.

Anna Karenina DVD. 50p.

Wales. Edward Thomas (1924) £5.

Concrete Poetry. ed. Stephen Bann (1967). 50p.

The Fables of Aesop and Others and Aesop's Fables
(Everyman; Penguin).

Tortilla Flat. John Steinbeck. Penguin.

The Kraken Wakes. John Wyndham. Penguin. £2 for 4.

The Farm and the Village. George Ewart Evans. £1.

FRIDAY 23RD JULY, 2021, HORSLEY CROSS.

Roy Leslie 78. 50p.

Clamps and box of rivets. £3.

(unknown item). 50p.

A Creel of Willow. W.H. Canaway.

Castles (East Anglia). HMSO.

Counties of England (2nd series) cards.

Plays. Chekhov. Penguin. 4 books for £2

New potatoes. £1.

In the cold days after Christmas, my harvest is to write about a sunny day of relaxed, good bargains, some surprising. I have already discussed the fiddle above, in Week 8, but it seemed to set the tone for the day. I was not resistant to quality – for example in buying the Edward Thomas where I disobeyed my rules for keeping to cheap books – if I found a lovely book with good illustrations. And the Aesop with other fables felt like a real find, which I intend to keep. But one book took me by surprise.

I saw the *Concrete Poetry* book and thought little of it. It was ex-library, always a killer of value, and a bit tatty. But, as I looked at it, I thought, "Present for Phil." So this happened. Phil is Philip Terry, Professor in the Department of Literature Film and Theatre Studies at the University of Essex and my colleague and friend of some 20 years. It's been said that he is the person making current, experimental poetry accessible to all. Phil and I have always been respectful opposites, even complementary ones, in both senses. I am an old traditionalist folkie, he is a modernist punk. We are like rockers and mods, or trad and cool jazz, where he is cool and I'm not.

The strange thing is, we meet in our regard for the old stuff. Specifically, by co-incidence, like Aesop. The first of Phil's work I read were his versions and deviations of Aesop, of which he has published two books. I have and like both. He also edited a brilliant book of versions of Ovid tales, *Ovid Metamorphosed*. This became a set text for first-year literature students.

When I got home that Wednesday, I looked up the books I had bought on the internet, as I often do. *Concrete Poetry*, I was amazed to find, even in its tatty, ex-library state, had value. The cheapest one online was even tattier and was offered for more than £150. The most expensive offered was in the States and was over £500. Of course, you should always take internet prices with some scepticism. All they indicate is potential value, not real value. If you look at the completed listings page of eBay, for example, you can see what price an item actually sold for. I took the book over to Bookshop Dave on the Saturday and we pondered it. We agreed that if we wanted to sell it, a London dealer might give us £50, if we were lucky. I am even more convinced of this now, as the copies I saw online are still there, offered at the same price, six months later. I said to Dave, "I reckon I'll give it to Phil, as I intended in the first place."

We both thought it a really interesting item. We noted it had been in the Colchester Institute library, when it was called the North East Essex Technical College. I did a pre-degree Access course there and had fond memories of the library. It was in a purpose-built tower-like building, with spacious staircases and lovely places to sit by windows and felt friendly and well-designed.

A couple of years later, I was in a pub in Castle Hedingham, chatting to a chap in a tweed suit about education. He asked me if I had used the library, when I mentioned going to the Institute. I said I had and he asked me what I thought of the building. I innocently expressed my admiration for it. "That's the right answer," he said, "I was the architect." I said I was pleased to be able to tell him how much I liked it. Recently, of course, it has been demolished and some horrible block of neo-liberal industrial brutalism has replaced its concrete poetry with drab utility.

Anyway, I phoned Phil, to see if he already had the book. He asked me to hang on a minute. He then found a photocopy of the Introduction, made for him by Professor Dawn Ades, an expert on Dada and surrealism from our neighbouring Art History department at Essex. He hadn't got the book and would like it. I told him of its origin and he reminded me that his mum, Molly, who I knew, used to work there as a librarian. Incidentally, she had also worked with Philip Larkin as a fellow librarian at Belfast. We decided that the book was even more his: "It's *your* book," I said.

It also had to be the book of the year, I had already decided, as it was not only of interest and valuable, at least potentially, and at least rare, but spoke of its and our times. Strangely, I think I even remember it coming out in 1969. It was at this time I used to visit Better Books, just off Charing Cross Road in London, which was the hippest poetry bookshop in London. My girlfriend Pat and I would buy Ginsberg's work there and look at the new books. Experimental poetry existed in 60s London alongside the beats and those they influenced. We went to readings where Mike Horowitz and Adrian Mitchell read alongside Bob Cobbing, who was a sound poet. Bob Cobbing ran Better Books. I'm sure we looked at the anthology, one of the first of its kind of shaped poetry, when it came out, probably while buying our copy of *International Times*.

One of the first things I ever published was in that hippy magazine. I wrote an article about acoustic music for their music section, in the brief era they had one, around that time.

I met Phil for lunch soon after and, nicely, Dawn Ades also happened to be on the TV that evening, in a programme called *How to be a Surrealist*, fronted by Phillipa Perry. Everything was connected, which made the book about the shape of poetry even more shapely. At the same time, Phil gave me a gift of his new book, a miniature (see week 11), called *Birds of the British Isles*.

The cards from the 1930s, of English counties, are offered for around £30 and they are quality too and a complete set. This series two is of the Midlands. The cards could be framed, if laid side by side. They are beautiful but remain with me, as I am not sure who would like them. I seek someone who has some of the others in the series but lacks this set, in its box, as made by Jaques of London. I might give them to my great nephew Scott, as even at 12 he has an eye for old things. He recently bought a book from a charity shop, because of its age and leather binding. He showed us it at the Christmas dinner table. It happened to be poems by Mathew Arnold and the poor lad had to endure me reading Dover Beach aloud. My niece Anna commented that it was a dark thing to write on your honeymoon, as Arnold is said to have done. But he does also say "let us be true to one another". Anyway, Scott might like the cards for his old and interesting department one day.

Bought for myself was another Roy Leslie 78, on the Eclipse label. These small 78s were for sale in Woolworth's for 6d, so I am told. Woolworth's, now long gone, was the Wilko or Poundland of its day. Great for fun and for cheap stuff and for children to find bargains in, although they were a joke, too. The Eclipse label had lots of comic songs which are now collectable. I have always sought the old stuff through boot sales, especially my collection of comic song 78s, which inspire me so. This is not nostalgia or, at least, not just nostalgia. These guys were up to date in their own way and social commentators on their own times. They had workable ways of writing about the now, which we don't have so readily, I think.

My interest in these old arts can look like being at odds with the modern world, but although I reserve the right to remain in that box, it's not so simple as that. My delving into the forgotten has a point, I hold.

I suppose my first boot sale harvest was compiling a CD of 78s I had bought, for my own pleasure. I have a record deck for 78s, bought from a mail order firm that specialised in stuff for oldies like me back then – and maybe more so then than now, when I actually qualify as one. A lead goes from the record deck to a mini-jack into a digital recorder, thence onto CD, to play in the car. Nowadays this tech is redundant, but it still works and my car still has a CD player. I made three CDs in all, shared with a few interested friends. The first two were comic and old commercial cowboy stuff, with a few folk dance tunes and Max Bygraves novelties, and the third was folk dance tunes, which I titled Folky McFolkface. The other two were called Scratched to Fuck and Bootsale Bonanza. We used to sing along with them, me and my last girlfriend. The only parallel you could find today is Barry Humphries' occasional shows on Radio 2 of Forgotten Musical Masterpieces. Owning your influences has always been important.

Among the songs were things I only knew from my dad singing them, remembered from his youth. 'The Last of the Texas Rangers', for example. It is amazing how the whole cowboy thing took over the world, or the fantasy world of men of the previous generation. Everyone seemed to dream of American hope in their hearts and American romanticism has not gone away, as we know. The potent mythologies of the Wild West, with its over-simplifications and elaborations, work still. My favourite film is often on TV, where Kirk Douglas plays a cowboy stranded in a meaningless modern world. He is the mythological against the mechanical, dehumanised world, in *Lonely are the Brave*.

The cowboy songs of the past were not entirely aimed at fantasy either. Many of them came from the same sources as the blues and country and they reflected the poverty of the times and could encompass anything, even their own critique. Country music is still uneasy about Carson Robison (see last week) but I like his stuff for its awkward fit.

My hero Leslie Sarony wrote 'Jollity Farm' as a response to an American depression song he covered, 'Misery Farm'. The English silly defiance this showed became very important to me, early on. He wrote protest songs too, about the tearing down of old buildings in London. He also appeared in plays by Samuel Beckett during the 1970s, where the character lives in a dustbin, and told reporters of an old song of his about dustbins. He was more present than any nostalgia slot on TV might have allowed.

Phil Terry edited the recent *Penguin Book of Oulipo*, an anthology of experimental writing which seeks new or different forms or formal constraints for writing. Phil also teaches this kind of approach. In many ways, my seeking out of the music hall, variety, cowboy songs and folk tunes and songs is a similar seeking of forms that make useful sense to a writer. I do not feel averse to any formal investigations.

These things meet usefully in the *The Fables of Aesop and Others* book. I was drawn to the 'other' ones, some from Indian sources especially. Phil was very inventive in using Aesop, so they seem both old and very new. This book, an Everyman paperback, ties in well with my harvest as it has a postscript by Roger Lancelyn Green, he of the first book I found this year. The book is a 1973 reprint of an Everyman from 1913, edited by Ernest Rhys. My bookmark, from July, is on a tale from 'Pilal' (India), called 'The Nightingale and the Countryman', where the bird seems more sophisticated than the human. It is not merely a clash between nature and culture, although it partly is.

The man cultivates roses and sees the bird taking part of his favourite flower. He then catches the bird and puts it in a cage. The bird tells him he will be punished for his cruelty in the 'other world', so the man sets the bird free.

The bird then rewards him by telling him where to look for buried treasure. He finds it, but is puzzled. He asks why the bird did not escape his net, if he can know where treasure is hidden. The bird tells him that we cannot escape our fate, however clever. The bird then makes reference to other tales but says "what once befell the Hunter will be his destiny". At the end of the tale we are not even sure it is not the tale-teller who speaks, though through the bird. There is a strange intimacy of the two points of view, where desire and desire for freedom are balanced and put into their place by nature. These balances of knowing and unknowing are only balanced through the tale itself, through both innocence and experience. Under a page and a half long, it's such a complicated, simple fable.

I find the new in the old and the old in the new, stepping out of time here to take the tenor of the times. The old stuff gives me a lens, a form and makes me more present. This whole project is a stereoscopic triangulating lens to locate myself in my culture. It would be good if I had bought a stereoscope, but I think you might see such a thing at an antique market but less likely at a boot sale.

As I said, Phil and I are opposites. When another friend and colleague who knows us both well, asked me if Phil and

I were close, I said, "Close, but not adjacent, if you see what I mean." He did.

S.J. Perelman is a good case (see Week 3). His comic columnist's writing, though popular, was hugely experimental, in 1930s–1950s America. James Joyce was his hero. Frank Muir devotes a significant section of *The Oxford Book of Humorous Prose* (1990) to Perelman. I recently mended the torn dust jacket of *The Most of S.J. Perelman* and might even give it to Phil one day.

The recent plague seems to me to have put us so much back into the logical conclusion of our selfishness. So it feels all the more important to take ourselves out of our eternally vigilant present, feeling sympathy for those that ignore it and trying out the forgotten forms of the world, where the rare book springs to life, when read, valuable beyond its value. Like the moralising nightingale, we can be wise beyond our limits as bird or as captured bird. 'The Countryman and the Nightingale' comes originally from a book called *Tales Within Tales*, I think.

Over the last couple of years, I have bought Punch and Judy material too, as more of my interest in old forms. I also used to pick up 1930s books by Walter Wilkinson, himself a Punch and Judy man, who created popular tales of his travels and performances. I liked the primitive symbolism of the old characters. They still contained laughs and I do remember seeing them on beaches as a child, silly and violent as the stories were. But it was funny, inventive and the whole world in miniature and the men, called Professors, who performed it, fascinated me. The strange voice of Mr Punch, made by the use of a swozzle, was strange, comic and other, as we might say. They were archaic and adaptable and seemed a self-contained otherworld and to hold some psychological truth. In other words, they were fully mythic.

Once, in Brighton, there was an old booth and set of puppets for sale in a junk shop and my friend Bob and I discussed buying them and becoming Punch and Judy men. We were serious, but guessed our business sense, which was zero, would count against us. Punch and Judy men were buskers and one of them had to bottle, which means collect money from the crowd.

I bought two modern puppets: one of the Crocodile and one of Mr Punch. These were modern but good, and I like puppets, even if I have never really used them myself. A few weeks later I came across an old carved frieze on a panel, obviously from a real Punch and Judy act. These two buys sit together, where they can be seen. When I set them up, I immediately thought of writing something called 'Living with the Crocodile', which my Mr Punch seemed to be reduced to. I resolved to watch Tony Hancock's masterpiece, usually dammed by listings people as no good, *Punch and Judy Man*, an existential epic film which Hancock part-wrote, and which is sometimes still shown on TV. It had the required mix of hope amid despair at the world, which is the showman's fate.

The Fable of Mr Punch and the Crocodile today seems a

better title for my puppets:

MR PUNCH AND THE CROCODILE

"Where are the Sausages, the Baby, the Policeman, and where is Judy?" asked the Crocodile, counting the missing on his four feet, although in fact he had no feet, only cloth, which seemed to hide, or not hide, fingers.

Mr Punch didn't answer straight away. Then, he looked towards the Crocodile slowly and said: "And where is my Stick?"

"I was hoping to forget your Stick," said Croc.

"Tradition gave me a stick, a club, a staff," said Punch, a little sadly.

There was a pause.

Then the Croc said: "We are the masculine remains of an out-of-date form, with no use or purpose left."

"I could make a useful purse out of you!" Mr Punch suddenly chirped up.

There was another useful pause.

"It's no good making old-style jokes at my expense. Even your name is aggressive, like your jokes. At least I'm just an animal."

"In fact, we're both puppets, as you know. You did the joke of counting on your fingers, breaking the fourth wall. Maybe we should retreat into the booth in the rain and try to retain our enigma, our heritage status."

"We've proved we can make jokes out of anything. We

could pretend to have a fight. I could pretend I thought you were Judy."

"Or I could pretend I thought you were," said Croc.

"There's nothing to fight over. If we just do our jokes, Judy might come back," said Mr Punch.

"Maybe you killed the Policeman and Judy. And ate the Sausages."

Mr Punch replied: "Maybe you ate the Baby!" Then he paused again. "No," he said, "the Baby and Judy and the Policeman and even the Sausages are still out there somewhere. All we can do is wait and try to make some interesting jokes and pauses, and the odd copper."

"Increase, Love, Justice, and Nourishment are no mean things," said the Croc, portentously. Mr Punch looked at him, surprised.

"And my staff is my burden," he added, sadly.

With that, the Policeman peeped round the curtain, but proved to be just a helmet with a hand in it.

[Curtain.]

A few years further back, I bought two old music hall posters from the Empire, Edmonton. My mum lived in Edmonton and used to play the theatre organ. One of these posters, from 1910, features the surreal, non-smiling comic song man, Sam Mayo. He is top of the bill. These hang in my kitchen. They were a bargain. Because of his name and his dourness, I imagine him writing a song called 'Me and the Crocodile', with lines about making it snappy, and missing his staff, all delivered in his characteristic mock-dull style, like his bill-matter says, as "the man who refuses to smile" and "The Sombre One".

Week 14: NOTEBOOKS

WEDNESDAY 28TH JULY, 2021. MARKS TEY.

Rivets. £2.

The L-Shaped Room. Lynne Reid Banks. 50p.

DVDs about Billy Bragg and Steve Earle. £2.

Robert Burns plate. £1.50.

The Threepenny Novel. Bertolt Brecht (Penguin).

Sea Magic.

Blue leather writing case. 3 items for £3.

Old briefcase. £2.

Bald violin bow. £2.

Staple gun with staples. 50p.

Selected Poems. Ted Hughes. 20p.

Leather-bound notebook. 50p.

I just walked over to a heap of notebooks at home, some new, some gifts but mostly bought new or secondhand, from boot sales. There must be 25 there, at a rough count, which seems enough. I do give them away occasionally but the fact remains that I can't resist a nice old notebook, or sometimes a nice new one. Ever since I was a child, I've loved a notebook and writing in one. I must have been 10 when I bought a small spiral notebook from Woolworths, which fitted neatly in my pocket. I liked its portability. There is too much to say about this most personal subject and I'm guessing that if you don't get it, this could be dull for you.

I do try to resist buying too many notebooks, but something a little different will always get me, like the leather-bound 4" x 7" one listed above (1½" thick), which was too good to miss at 50p; or the one I just retrieved from the heap (of shame? Not really). It looks like a Bible, with gold-edged pages and two ribbon bookmarks attached. It has 'Believe' embossed into the leather on the front and more legend underneath, which I had to use a magnifying glass to read. So far, so biblical. "I believe that the most beautiful thing is worth waiting (*sic.*) and the sweetest fruit needs patience," it says. Deciphering this, I guess it is a Bible of Self, or of self-improvement. They could start with the grammar: 'awaiting' might have been cool, as self-improvement sometimes goes for the archaic. A book in which to write self-affirmations. Any old catharsis is good though. It is all writing.

You can buy this notebook for £10.99 on the internet, I have just discovered. The pages are not lined. I would never have bought it new, as it does not feel writing-friendly to me. Might be a good sketchbook. I may well end up giving it away as a gift, as it feels substantial and the cover is good leather.

While I've always liked notebooks (and especially 'rough books' at school), before I was 22 I usually wrote on any paper, in the kind of Hank Williams' shoe-box random method. My friend Fiona, who kept a journal, persuaded me that hardbacked notebooks were better, as you could find things and that dating writing was good, too. What I feared was that, if I returned to something I had written in a notebook and it made me feel sick, I wouldn't want those words near any new writing. I didn't want bad writing to infect potentially good writing, so I'd always go to a fresh piece of paper. "You just turn the page," she said.

In those days, we were sharing a flat in London and I occasionally used to go to Foyles in Charing Cross Road to buy books. Foyles also had a really good selection of notebooks. I liked A4 size, with narrow lines (feint-ruled) and margins. Since then, I've always had a current hardback notebook on the go. My present one is an old, blue, faded, boot-sale buy, with the old money price of 2/9 (about 14p) written in pencil on the first page. Someone had used a page at the back, also in pencil. It has been a nice companion over the last two years. Everything is in there, even my logs for this project. I only have a few pages left, so soon I will have the pleasure of choosing a new one. I don't think it will be 'Believe', the solipsist's bible, though maybe that's what I deserve.

Often on a book project I do have another, smaller notebook going, just for book notes. At present, it is the green exercise book, bought in the first week from Horsley Cross, which seemed appropriate. There are a couple of other notebooks, bought over the summer. One is the mini-ring binder, as discussed in week 11 and I think there is another exercise book coming up, albeit an old one. Old stationery often has better quality paper, to be savoured.

If I look up at the top of the bookshelf in front of me, I can also see my collection of office equipment. Hole-makers, staplers, numerators, an antique guillotine, the above staple-gun and two stone bottles of red ink. Nearly all these are from boot sales. The big stone bottles of red ink I bought from my own charity shop warehouse. 'BRILLIANT RED' they say, 'WRITING INK', Philip and Tacey, Ltd, 69-79 Fulham High Street, London SW6. They have sealed stoppers and one even has some of the original corrugated cardboard packaging, tied with string, round its neck. They must have been for accountancy, the other great use of writing, or writing's dull brother. There is no accounting for taste; in my case no taste for accountancy. The ink of correction, brilliant red for outstanding debt. Typewriters must have put Philip and Tacey out of business, albeit with red ribbons. They are a cool item. Checking online, I think Philip and Tacey might have been educational suppliers, so the writing connection is more prominent. For correction, for inkwells.

I have never been tempted to open one of these, but if

I see ink in small bottles, I often buy it. I have a drawer full of old dipping ink-pens and bottles of ink and I once wrote a novel with dip-pen. At school, a friend and I used dip-pens, as the ink-wells were still there in our classroom desks, though rarely used. We were retro even then. We felt the thoughtful and inscribed were better quality in dip-pen writing. We were an anomaly. I rarely use them now, but I still keep them. I also have a John Bull Printing Outfit or two lying about.

Are these 'sad secrets', as one of my students used to say, or are they indicative of something else? So far, so much just about things. I feared this book being merely about things. Then, when I thought about it and looked at my buying log, I realised it wasn't so. All these things are there for creative purposes. Everything I buy has to feed me creatively. That is my aesthetic, I guess.

Also, these things are displacement objects too. I have noticed that I buy guitars when I can't think of anything to play, for a crude example. But they all incline me towards maintaining my creative life. Even the rivets, listed above. I made a belt loop with them to keep my trousers up. Making it myself was an act of self-maintenance, like writing has always been, and is especially now in older age.

There is mending and there are stimulating objects and there are old notebooks awaiting their destiny as writing tools. Only the stone jars of ink speak of useless ornaments. Sometimes I do buy useless things. I couldn't resist the old blue writing case, but I now think it's beyond use. It has airmail paper, also blue, in it. Maybe for writing to an old lover abroad. I don't know why I bought it as its use has not suggested itself, but it is forgivable in its appeal to old writings, old connections.

I rarely use any non-boot-sale handwriting equipment these days except for uni-ball Impact pens, which replaced the unobtainable Zebra 2000 in my affections. This is only when I'm not using fountain pens and ink, rarely bought new.

I do miss Woolworths, which was a place where children felt at home and prices were low. I realised in the 1970s that certain cash books were song-shaped – longish and narrow so good for writing lyrics in. When I realised things were changing at Woolworth and the stores were gradually going, I bought a few of their own-brand cash books to keep me in stock. Seeing that I rarely made a living from songs, I also enjoyed the amusing proximity between poetry and economics. I still have two of the cash books left. They were 75p each. They are about 5" wide, by 11" high, code S630. I would often paint the blue cover with black enamel, to cover the 'winfield' and 'CASH BOOK' headlines. I would copy completed songs from the bigger notebooks, or even compose direct into them. I think I should use them soon, lest they outlast me.

My love of old stationery is a large and personal thing. I used to look in bins and skips at the university for old folders and binders, especially springback ones, as everything became digitised and old stationery was ditched. Anything pre-plastic in the folder line is good. I use old, red ones for my songs these days, which were being dumped by my own university department.

I haven't counted how many notebooks I have filled, but they go back many years and live in a big blanket box, which is my archive. Choosing a new one is a serious business, as they often last a few years. The current blue one goes back to October 2019. The previous one was a new one, though bought at a boot sale – a big A4 Red and Black Oxford with narrow feint and margins. I always stick a bit of ribbon in with PVA glue for a bookmark. This makes finding a new page to get an idea down very quick. The next one could be smaller or larger, depending on mood. I now like the old books best.

At Marks Tey maybe eight or 10 years ago I found two big notebooks, which must have been drugs books from Severalls Mental Hospital, recently closed, I guessed. The top of each blank page had 'DANGEROUS DRUGS' printed at the top. I had to send one to my pal Bob, who had a lifelong experimental interest in drugs and was also a poet. The notebooks cost me £2 each and quite a bit more to post one, but one went to Bob and I hope he used it. I could use the other one next, as a tribute to Bob, who died recently, though these days poetry is my only dangerous drug. When the last pages of the old book are full, I will enjoy deciding. In fact, my laptop rests on a big hardbacked notebook, thick and of some antiquity, which I could use. It is a heavy old thing though, but still. But it won't be the 'Believe' notebook, I believe.

Though I have not even covered how I like American notebooks and three-ring binders and have even asked friends to find them for me when visiting the States, I fear that this chapter is too personal and trivial. I must make the next one different, but I also feel I must include here the song I wrote about this topic, called Stationery-o-file.

I've got a secret vice though it's not nasty
A craving that has experts at a loss
It's not for kinky clothes, nor things that your Mum loathes
No types of dressing that would make her cross
But like a demon it wells up as if it really was
Something to be ashamed of though I'm not at all because

I'm a stationery-o-file, biros are the only thing I'm biting
Nice ring-binders make me smile, eraser is the rubber
    that's exciting
I know it's not disastrous if you buy an extra pen
But I've got forty in my drawers, because I can't say when
On paper I am innocent, though I've stolen quite a pile
I'm a stationery-o-file

I've got a secret vice, it's no perversion
Stationery's what moves me most I guess

I wasn't teacher's pet, though I dogged her you bet
Into the old stock cupboard I confess
It's not paper underwear that makes me beg for more
But I'd crawl across the floor for a nice piece of A4

Chorus

I've got a secret vice though it's not sordid
Still the lure of it I can't explain
Do pens have potency? Paper, fecundity?
Or is it that I'm just slightly insane?
So take a leaf from my book, have a refill, it's no sin
I'm going to hide in Ryman's and I hope they lock me in

Chorus

(I hang round typing pools/ Get off me rollerballs)

There are some things that are dated here, obviously, but it was a good one to do unaccompanied with my friend Elaine in two-part harmony. It usually led to confiding confessions from audience members, so I know I am not alone.

Notebooks can remain unused and you never know who might finally write enough to fill one. They are a kind of hope of reflection and have a presence that print-outs and files don't have. Now I don't mind the bad writing being so near to the good writing in an everyday notebook. Nothing you write is wasted and there are riches there for me, which is the everyday wishes of the writer to say the thing that will wing its way to another ear. I doubt my old papers will be preserved, as I am not successful enough to be archived, but I can archive myself as an act of self-respect, confession or prayer.

There are four notebooks bought this year. The new, green exercise book I am using, the one Self-Bible bought this week, a small hardback Collins 418, bought in Week 11 and one more in the penultimate week of the season. This one, costing all of 10p, is another exercise book, with a beige cover, of some age. It is a Stationery Office government issue book with a crown on the cover, emblazoned 'S.O. Book 609'. It has 80 pages, also mentioned on the cover, and narrow feint, which I prefer. As the last of a season in which I showed remarkable restraint, I think it has chosen itself for my next main notebook. It is small, portable and no threat in size or number of pages. It has the ring of the end of the season. It has age, even though it is not worn out. I feel it is perfect. I might well do a bit of free-drafting in the old book to get to it and choose a book mark or ribbon to wed to it – maybe use a paper clip, for the new minimalism.

It is not a hardback, though, but I can break my rule for the sake of lightness and timeliness.

Among the notebooks I didn't buy this year was a big accounts book, unused, with a lock and key, which would have amused me, but it came under the label of intimidating due to its size, price and self-importance.

Why is this all so personal? Well, I suppose it's because this is where I live, scribbled into my books of life. And computers are often, for me, just fancy notebooks of the disappearing kind, so not as close to life.

So, it's 10p for my future. I love blank pages where I can feint, in the sense of making a gesture of attack, along the feint, in the sense of lines. The place of infinite suggestion and open horizon. I don't know if the Stationery Office still do notebooks, but they still do Hansard and my notebook will contain riches, doings and beginnings as well as endings, on old, thick paper, pleasingly aged. Make your own jokes.

Week 15: BAD POETRY

WEDNESDAY 4TH AUGUST 2021. MARKS TEY.

Medieval English Lyrics. ed. R.T. Davies. £1.

England, England. Julian Barnes. 50p.

To Jerusalem and Back. Saul Bellow. 50p.

The Making of the English Landscape. W.G. Hoskins. 50p.

The Priestley Companion. Penguin, £1.

The Ginger Man. J.P. Donleavy. £1.

The Bayeaux Tapestry. King Penguin. £1.

In the Steps of George Borrow. Eileen Bigland. £1.

The Stuffed Owl. ed. D.B. Wyndham Lewis and Charles Lee. 50p.

Elizabethan Mansions. King Penguin. £1.

Cambridge. King Penguin. £1.

McDougall's English Songster. Edward Mason. £1.

English Folk Songs for Schools. Sabine Baring Gould and Cecil Sharp. £1.

This week I only bought books – and quite a few of them will be bound straight for Dave's bookshop, like the King Penguins. But the two folk song books, bought last, and the odd but well-known anthology *The Stuffed Owl* (of 'Bad Verse') and the book of medieval lyrics all remind me of differing views of poetry. The other book I want to refer to here was not bought until later (week 17), but that is John Betjeman's *Sweet Songs of Zion*, which is a celebration of hymn writers or hymnodists, to use that unfamiliar but cheerful term. All these make me think of useful poetry as a good thing, rather than the high-art view of art as a separate thing with rules of its own.

Being myself a lyric writer and performer helps me to incline towards the utility of the lyrical being the key to its strengths as well as its weaknesses. Attending funerals this year too reminded me that some poetry is useful but not necessarily good. I don't mind this myself and do not fear the incontinence of writing as a danger. This, it seems to me, as a person who taught in a literature department of a university for many years, is what those fear who have only taught what is accepted as the best. I always found that the older teachers, and those who taught older literature, had more tolerance of creative work of any kind than the critics and theorists who mostly looked down on the whole thing, as an elaboration of the snobbery of the purists who only liked the accepted greats.

It always has seemed to me that there is an undercurrent of useful verse in the world. It is often simpler, often more old-fashioned, often used and passed on, and it runs counter to literary fashion or the cheese-paring of expert litterateurs. I align myself with this, despite having "been with the professors" (although it wasn't always, in my experience, that they "liked your looks). I'm quoting their often-cited exception-maker Bob Dylan here. An anthology of 'bad Dylan' lines is an easy project. But the fact remains that Dylan is still almost universally popular in literature departments. He is their exception and also their double standard.

The Stuffed Owl, which ran to many editions, stands as a reminder of both literary snobbery and of the endurance of the useful over the beautiful. The edition I bought is the 'Further Enlarged' edition of 1948, following the first edition of 1930 and the 'enlarged' of the same year. Few poetry books run to that many versions, but I despise the book. The introduction reads today like a parody of bad criticism, with its extreme, superior snobbery on show. Also, it is no longer funny, almost without exception. What were they laughing at here? It is mostly impossible for me to see what is 'bad', in their terms. Ideas of bad change quicker than ideas of what is good, and I am pleased I cannot see what the editors are on about, as they nudge away at the reader. I shall pass this book on soon.

As someone who loves traditional song, I am familiar with going through so much stuff that doesn't appeal in order to find the killer lines that do. This is a process of getting into the minds of the old writers, often of anonymous folk and ballad poetry. You find the useful stuff and work out from that. This, I used to tell students, was inductive rather than deductive criticism. You find a small bit that works for you like a key and then move from there to see the whole. The deductive critic looks from outside with a theory of what literature is and tries to impose it from above. The writer must, to be useful and to find poetry useful to herself, work from what is useful. It is a positive aesthetic and one of utility and appreciation towards the most genuine attempts of communication. This way of working is not averse to simplicity or to real human feeling. Poetry is not a symptom of something else, it is the currency of the everyday.

It is in the out-of-fashion kinds of books you regularly find at boot sales that you can find the old corny truths of humanity. The sentiment of a time tells you much about the time. Those old songs, both 'soppy' and 'stern' let you see into your parents' day, as Larkin had it. In his *Required Writing*, he tells of a competition he was asked to judge, where they had removed, to his displeasure, all the love poetry and all the nature poetry. The snobberies of the day pass away quickly, though I am pleased to say that the nature stuff, as fashionable now, at least, would be in.

The J.B. Priestley anthology is better value and a keeper, for me. The title of 'companion' echoes one of his best novels, *The Good Companions*. He is often seen as 'middlebrow' and not for literature departments, but I am a fan of his *Literature and Western Man*, where his diagnosis of what is wrong with modern literature still stands. He says that there is an emphasis on decline in the modern, which neglects real human value and results in a separation of art from life. This year, as I write, 2022, there is much discussion of so-called 'modernism' with it often said to have started around 100 years ago. Much of the best of modernism, for me, was a new traditionalism. Much of the worst was mere snobbery and fascism, which, incidentally, was not that new either. 'Modernisn't' is my own word for this, and the experimental is not the exclusive realm of the 20th century, either.

I remember reading an interview with a 'prize-winning' poet a while ago, which always makes me wonder if there are any other sort. I am maybe a 'prize-free' poet. Anyway, he said poetry these days is either over-simple or beyond comprehension and how he hates light verse. It seems to me that he has missed something of the root of poetry, the song in the street lyricism that must carry all poetry if it is to pass Adrian Mitchell's test of not ignoring 'most people'. You do not have to look far to find lyricism. Finding your own seems harder.

Medieval English Lyrics has loads of memorable and singing phrases in the old poet's hymns on love, death and God. "When my eyes are misting / And my ears are full of hissing" is a modern version of 'How Death Comes'. It is funny, gloomy and lyrical and somehow triumphant in its lightness in the face of death. At the end, it is as startling as any shock poem: "On my nose my house will sit / For the whole world I don't give a shit." This is my translation but I hope I have captured the triumph and defiance and the jaunty, chanty, hard nature of the old English lyricism.

W.H. Auden's anthology *The Oxford Book of Light Verse* (1938) insists that "light verse can be serious". "The problem for the modern poet, as for everyone else today, is how to find or form a genuine community," he writes in his introduction. Lightness, like lyricism, comes from community, from shared traditions. There are some here in these books, far away from the agonised, serious prize-winner.

English Folk Song for Schools starts with 'The Raggle-Taggle Gipsies, O!' It seems a loss that kids now probably do not know this song of transgression from the norm, where the Lady runs away with the gipsies. They wouldn't even appreciate Miles Wootton's parody, 'The Hippies and the Hairies, O!' "What makes you leave your house and land / Your washing machine and the stereo / ... to go with the hippies and the hairies, O!?" No-one could doubt the serious lightness here, or the lyricism, in the original or the parody.

Likewise, *McDougall's English Songster* begins with the corny old 'Begone Dull Care', with its lyrical personification, "Long hast thou been tarrying here / And fain you would me kill." I have never heard this sung, except as a joke, but I now think it is serious, light and lyrical. Both of these songs have folk-memory for me. Both I would love to hear sung sensitively and thus escape and find a confrontation with the dullnesses of life, into the shared and lyrical.

Like Auden, I am a fan of Thomas Moore, the Irish poet of many well-known lines. I have been known to sing his 'Minstrel Boy', as another song in need of rescuing from its obscurity, all the greater for its over-familiar corniness. I also sing 'Oft In the Stilly Night', which I learnt from a CD of Irish songs sung by John McCormack. I love this old stuff, it has a clarity unavailable to us now. This last I used to do as an encore in folk clubs, where rescuing old songs and recasting them was accepted and part of our tradition.

Hymns are another great source and have much cross-breeding with traditional tunes. Betjeman's *Sweet Songs of Zion* started as radio scripts. It would be better listened to, where one might hear the hymns, but, while the texts seem bitty and the hymns too long, there is much to enjoy in his book (bought Week 17). He has a genuine passion for the lyricisms which were being overlooked then, in the 1970s, as now.

It is not that I like everything, or think nothing is bad, but I resist others' definitions, as I suspect snobbery at work so often. I can forgive my own snobberies, I suppose. Someone gave me a book of a popular internet poet. The book was crowd-funded and although it is fine I don't like it much. It seems profuse and disconnected at times and maybe I prefer old stuff nowadays, since I no longer have to read students' work that much and confront their everyday good and bad.

Writers have to discriminate. We are discriminators. We have to choose one word over the other. Reading with positive prejudice is part of my method. But finding good in the forgotten is a happy thing. Six of the above bought books from the week have reminded me of this. The last one being the biography of George Borrow, who himself went off with the Raggle Taggle Gipsies. Eileen Bigland was a prolific author of her time and this book is from 1950. The opening scene is very strong. It is about the impression Borrow makes when arrives from his native Norfolk to visit relatives in Cornwall. Tall and black clothed, he comes from out of a snowstorm into a pub, where relatives are waiting, singing a greeting. He was already famous by this time as writer and friend of gipsies and he had walked 25 miles, as the coach was full. He makes a big entrance.

Borrow remains a controversial figure and, from this book, emerges as an awkward and difficult man, an outsider in the literary world, a poet whose poetry is rarely read. Larger than life and a pain, in short, but a talented one. As I read this book about him, I regretted not buying a few extra books of his I saw at an earlier sale.

There is a good poem of his quoted in the biography called 'The Wandering Children'. Here, the kids beg for money from a 'gentleman' who is full of moral cant, but offers them no sustenance. It is lyrical and even a bit shocking, but I wonder if it is in print anywhere else. There does seem to be a project to publish his poems and translations, though it is hard to find the contents of his many volumes of work, which look like pamphlets. There is no selected or collected poems, but he is a lyrical figure and *The Romany Rye* and *Lavengro* deserve their classic status; their titles meaning 'the gipsy gentleman' and 'words-man'.

I remember Allen Ginsberg saying in an interview that

he wanted to read poets' rejected or suppressed poems, to find their real secrets. My friend Hilary Llewellyn-Williams used to get students to write a secret poem that would be shared anonymously with the group at the end of a course. These secret poems feel empowering and revelatory and sometimes the bad things one writes say much and can even be our favourite things, as if we were children, displayed on our own fridges, to be wondered over. There might be simplicity, naivety and disarming honesty here, as well as that unconscious thing that we might not even know ourselves.

Jazz and experimental writing both embrace mistakes as hidden intentions. That is almost a cliché, but sometimes true. Lyrical ambiguity is useful for poetry in every way, that is for sure. Stumbling into honesty has always been a part of the lyrical.

Last night was Burns' Night. 'A writer', as he described himself, was on TV, giving readings from Burns' letters that made a hypocrite of his fine feelings of love. For me, it demonstrated nothing except a kind of 'school of resentment' (Harold Bloom), and an easy pointing out of others' faults. Also here was the expectation that writers should not be like other human beings. "OK, mate, read us some of your own impeccable works," I felt like saying. This was contrasted with a famous American writer fawning and being fawned over by Burns' fans. This did at least respect the verse and we heard the great Dick Gaughan sing a few of Burns' best.

I wrote about Burns myself, published this time last year in *PN Review*, in a piece called 'An Englishman in Search of Robert Burns'. I pointed out that, in his devotion to the collecting of traditional songs and his own confluence with tradition, he was the great model for all the traditional-influenced writers – like Bob Dylan, who admires Burns greatly. I also pointed out that 'Auld Lang Syne' is itself a song about tradition, that has become traditional. This, for me, is a real prize and an extraordinary achievement.

My Burns plate, bought last week, is bone China, by Dunelm. Ever since starting to write about him I had been looking for a bit of Burns tourist ware to keep and I was delighted to find it, especially here in Essex. Burns is hard to read and can be ropey, but this does not diminish him at all, in my eyes.

Thomas Moore's *Irish Melodies* made his name, but James Joyce's favourite song of Moore's was from a collection called *National Airs* and is to a Scottish tune. 'Oft In the Stilly Night,' which I love, has some characteristic Scottish cadences but the words are a great summing up of feeling left behind by life in age, or experience. The bit Joyce liked is this: "I feel like one / Who treads alone / Some banquet hall deserted / Whose lights are fled / Whose garlands dead / And all but he departed." Is this bad, or corny? No, it is traditional alienation brilliantly illuminated. I don't think Joyce cared about its critical merit and neither do I. I have a biography of Moore and a complete poems, both from past boot sales, and I want to learn more of his songs.

J.B. Priestley wrote everything except poetry and started out as a critic, but in the anthology bought above, in this week, he writes well on simplicity, in an excerpt from his book *Delight*. Reiterating what he says in *Literature and Western Man* somewhat, he recounts a conversation where a young critic accuses him of being 'too simple'. Priestley says here that he strives to be like that and says it reveals a different attitude to writing in his work. Echoing Auden, quoted earlier, he sees his writing in a community context, not as 'introspection' and says "I want to write something that at a pinch could be read aloud in a bar-parlour". Simplicity is hard to do well, he asserts, but that is what he tries for. In this he is with Burns, a traditionalist. Priestley is not much read nowadays but he is poetic and readable and often you can find his stuff at neglected stalls and charity shops, as I did.

I remember seeing the US singer Eric Von Schmidt in a Soho folk club in the late 1960s or early 70s. You might remember him, mentioned as 'Rick Von Schmidt' by Bob Dylan on his first LP. 'Rick' had no qualms about being a traditionalist blues man, concerned with the everyday lyricisms of blues. When he came back on for the second set, he said, "Someone just told me all my songs sound the same. It took me *years* to get 'em like that!"

This felt to me like a noble aim, to be like the great blues men, whose work resonated and reflected the everyday life they lived. Their work was beyond good or bad, it was part of them, it was them, and thus complete while remaining open to their times and community. It was a way of being in the world, not in spite of its contingencies or accidents, but accepting them in public art. Introspection and novelty were not so important.

'Errancy' is a term used to discuss an opposite of the rational in the contingent, the accident, the shadow of rational progress, in James Hillman's *Re-Visioning Psychology* (1975). Here we encounter the Knight Errant archetype, who must embrace his badness, his erring, his error. I could say 'her' here but didn't like to; it wasn't a mistake. While I read this in bed, I remembered a poem about a poet I wrote, called 'Poems', from *An Essex Attitude* (2009):

Heard a poet reading
you might know him
the intro was better
than the poem

everything in things
what a waste
it was clever and cleverer
but po-faced

things and abstracts
purblind verse
how I longed
for something worse

self-seeking flow
or constipated mutter

I long for some other
kind of nutter

I like poems
I don't want to suffer
I hark for something truer
deep, simple – rougher

Is that bad enough? I am happy too I can find echoes in
the medieval lyrics book, like 'I Must Go Walk the Wood So
Wild'. Here a heartbroken man wanders off, as in the more
recent traditional song 'Spenser the Rover', and as I feel I
have done myself for lost love, but to the boot sale instead.
"I must go to the old boot sale / And wander here and there
/ And throw off my despair / Where once love grew I fail /
And all for one / And all for one / And all for love of one."
This is how my version of lyric 154 might go, from about
the year 1500, more than 600 years ago and still touching
my heart with its bad.

Week 16: BRICOLAGE

FRIDAY 13TH AUGUST 2021. HORSLEY CROSS.

Singing Together. 50p.

Roberts radio. £2.

Dada and Surrealism. Dawn Ades.

The Rings of Saturn. W.G. Sebald.

Prehistoric and Roman Essex.

Rural Life in Victorian England.

Churches and Cathedrals. Puffin Picture Book.

5 books for £1.

Letters from London. Julian Barnes. 50p.

Strawberries. £1.20.

SATURDAY 14TH AUGUST 2021. BRAINTREE.

Anglepoise lamp. £4.

2 Roots Manuva CDs. 50p.

Rock Bottom. Michael Odell. 50p.

Envelopes. 50p.

It is not only the pleasures of wonderings and wanderings, but also their implications, that interest me most in my ritual boot-going. To that extent, this week I'm including epigraphs written as they have occurred to me now, as I'm writing my harvest reflections, rather than during the week in which an item was bought.

The first epigraph carries on from last week and is about bricolage.

"...a deviant perspective reflecting the deviance of the world. The psychological mirror that walks down the road, the Knight Errant on his adventure, the scrounging rogue, is also an odd-job man, like Eros the carpenter, who joins this bit with that, a handyman, a bricoleur... psychologising upon and about what is at hand; not a... planner with directions. And leaving, before completion, suggestion, an indirection, an open phrase..." (*Re-Visioning Psychology*, ch.3, James Hillman, 1976).

Is this what's actually happening here in this book, my journal of a bricoleur? My other epigraph is the aforementioned (in Week 3) from my mate Bob Hill, quoting the Highway Code: "Check for loose connections."

Bricolage is a French term that used to be architectural, but now means the artistic throwing together of disparate things. In everyday French it has become equivalent to DIY. Bricole means to cause to rebound. At its root is something like a bouncing war device and a kind of randomness of movement and discovery, while we seek loose connections that might become tight.

Anyway, this handyman bit is relevant here, as are the connections. It is against the law to sell electrical stuff untested for safety – so beware. You buy them at your own risk, I guess. We find the disparate things and throw them together in a festive bouncing, in the random volition of difference that accepts its connection. There is something of how the mind works here, interacting with the unpredictability of the world and answering its own questions.

There is a width in this connectedness with which we might try to join the writers who seem to have a universal 'spread', as poet Les Murray called it. Shakespeare and Dickens have big canvasses that seem to include everything. They are both serious and funny and have the quality of making stories cohesive and relatable, they have "bricolability" and the "pregnance" or "suggestful" quality of myth. The second of these is Hans Blumenberg, the third is mine, from *Myth and Creative Writing*.

I hope this is connective and that it works. The radio I bought does. My bathroom radio had packed up entirely. I expect young people do not have an old radio in their bathrooms, a bit dusty and needing batteries, in some corner, but it used to be that everyone needed one. I like to have one still. So, a radio from a stall for £2 was great. What is more, it was a Roberts with a mains lead. I sprayed the volume and tuning knobs with contact cleaner, cleaned the whole up with a mild disinfectant and warm water solution on a damp cloth and it works perfectly. I have just been listening to it. It did used to be a cassette player too, though it is small, but that bit doesn't work. As a kind of bonus, though, it has a cassette left in it, which I have left there, as a reminder of when I bought it.

The cassette is titled *Romantic Moments*. Sad that romance no longer plays. It makes me think of my artist friend Sarah and me at Weeley Boot Sale one year, when I discovered that my impression of Ralph Richardson made her giggle. We sat in the sun at a coffee stall, while I read aloud from a book I had just bought, in the voice of Ralph, making us both laugh and share that laugh with those around us. Maybe they were just being polite. No romantic moments playing out this year. The old cassette is in the old radio, just in case someone can renew the broken belt, or join the loose connection. Meanwhile the radio sounds good through its Roberts speaker, or do I mean Robert's, as in Bob of the connections?

At the same sale, I had a long chat with a family about two big double-cassette players they were selling. The dad told me they were his recording studio. I told him I had a similar machine in the 1980s, but of an inferior brand. His were top-of-the-range Sharp ones. Impressive 'ghetto-blasters'. He wanted 45 quid each for them and I was tempted to buy one, but resisted. The thing is, you could overdub from one cassette to the other, so you could do sound-on-sound multi-track recording. The ideal demo recording device – and having two must have been amazing, the equivalent of using Garageband or Audacity nowadays. He was probably doing dance beats in London, while I was overdubbing a concertina in Essex, but we laughed about it and admired the cherished machines.

I don't know if he sold them, but I do know modern bands and some fans like the retro sound of cassettes. My friend Martin Newell, who has a musical following in the States, still has cassettes available for that niche market. I did not mention my Pro Walkman, bought for £4, but cassettes were going round in my mind, despite the lack of romance.

The previous year had a particular highlight of a bargain, where I was actually looking for something, rather than just wandering. I usually have a mental list, on the look out for a particular small piece of practical use in the home. Once, when I asked a stallholder if he had any picture hooks, of the type you hang on picture rails, another customer produced one from his pocket, as if by magic and said, "Like this?" I agreed and he gave it to me.

I wanted a standing reading lamp for an old armchair in my office I had taken to using. I had covered it in a throw over its vinyl reupholstery and needed extra light. I cruised the field, looking at all the standard lamps I could see, which amounted to four or five. I saw a nice one, a bit like an Anglepoise on a stand, but the chap wanted £45 for it. I walked on, then decided, went back, and finally bought it for £38, having asked if he would do £35. He told me this lamp was a factory version of an Arne Jacobson design and that they were an expensive item. I did look this up and the cheapest new was about £70. On my way back to the car I stopped at the electrical man's stall and bought a spare light bulb for £2. It works grand.

An Anglepoise for £4 is a good price, although this one from Braintree is not in perfect condition it is usable and good. They get high money these days, but I must have bought at least four over the years. I also have a magnifying light of the kind used by people who sew, bought for a fiver and useful for cutting nails, finding splinters, doing small DIY and reading tiny print. I like the classic light, the Anglepoise, and have not bought any others than those above mentioned.

They are always turning other things into lamps on TV. "Look, I've made a lamp out of this lamp!" Not for me. People used to make lamps out of Mateus Rosé bottles, as a sign of sophistication. I recommend a cheap old Anglepoise, if you can find one, now they are deemed desirable.

I have already mentioned my big ladder in Week 2, but will return to it. I have bought book shelves, book cases, tools, notice boards, chairs, paint, glue, filler, hinges, clasps, a bicycle and an old wooden ashtray stand, which now is a cup stand by my armchair, as well as cigar boxes I gave to a ukulele maker and a couple I kept for pens. One friend asks me why my house is not full, but they go to Ikea regularly – and I have never been. I give much away and sometimes buy something big for a small part of it. Example: a mouldy and beyond-repair Gladstone bag. The bag itself went in the bin but the magnificent handle now adds value to a banjo-ukulele case I was giving to a pal. My place is a bit full, but mostly of guitars, ukes and books and no more full than it would be if I didn't go to boot sales.

The Dawn Ades book on surrealism, with 60 pages of paintings, went with Phil's book of the year to him (see Week 13). The *Singing Together* BBC schools booklet is from 1957 and contains 'The Minstrel Boy' mentioned last week, by Thomas Moore. I am not sure if my friend Elaine still collects these, but I will ask her. These books accompanied radio programmes for schools on the BBC radio Home Service. I remember them myself from my village school. However naff we felt this was, we did learn some folk songs and had them in common.

Many delicious things bought this week, especially the strawberries.

The Braintree sale was unusual, if small, but I found some interesting things, like the novel about rock journalism and the Roots Manuva CDs. It was £1 to enter, where the others I go to are 50p. I also fell into conversation with a musician who had a stall. I noticed he had some musical items and, although I bought none, we had a long chat about the local music scene and playing pro and semi-pro.

Colin from Danbury's dad was a double bassist and Colin had been a professional drummer. He got lots of work, as he could read music. He reminded me of my musical partner Murray, who plays bass. His dad was a drummer and Murray was doing gigs early. It was a week for chatting and I remember talking to the posh lady at Horsley Cross for the first time too, who I swear comes to the boot sale in a Bentley. She has the common touch and we have passed a few words many times since.

When I go to the Braintree sale, I always remember seeing my old guitar playing pal Malcolm Birch. Malcolm was always adapting old things into new with ingenious craftsmanship. I met him there by chance one day, long after we had been in a band together. Back when we were both in the Birch Brothers Band, he made me a case for my bass, which didn't have one. Then he made a big black box to fit on the ladder rack of my old Morris Minor van, for when we did trio gigs in pubs, in the 1970s. This had all the leads and mics in and was referred to as 'the coffin'. Malcolm was the prime bricoleur really, very handy and inventive, seeing possibilities, good at arranging and avoiding the normal world. He was offered a solo recording contract by a big company once, but got drunk and told them to F off. He was very Braintree. A sweet and bright man; much loved.

I always think of my time there when I go to that boot sale. Malcolm was a brilliant guitarist, subtle in a world of unsubtlety and a loss to many of us. His brother Nigel is still singing and plays a banjo-uke of the East German kind already visited in Week 8, which was the instrument bargain of the year in 2020. The rock journalism book was not great, really, as the main character seemed obsessed with the great stars being rebel anarchists and could not get over his disappointment. He should have known Malcolm, or Colin the drummer, and got a more humble idea of the bricolage of local music, subtler and often better than the grand, fallen heroes that disappointed him so.

As I mentioned in Week 2, I have a deep stairwell, going from the ground floor up to the first and second floors of my maisonette. To decorate this, you need a long ladder. The previous decorator had lost their nerve, as the paint didn't go right up to the ceiling. I looked up the cost of hiring a ladder and it was around £80 minimum. I wasn't expecting to find one at the boot sale, but I did.

A retiring builder was selling off some stuff, including a 30-foot ladder in two sections. He had a small pick-up van. I asked him how much and if he could deliver. He said £35 and he could deliver if I left a £10 deposit. I left him with my address. He delivered and I paid him the rest.

Sarah stayed with me when I went up and did the very top of the stairwell and it still looks OK today, albeit with a green giant Wilmington-style man painted on (see Week 2). I thought I might sell the ladder to the reclaim place down the road, but found that it would fit along the wall of my biggest attic room, which is 16-feet long. I am now glad I kept it, as it has been used a couple of times since, including last summer. I still have it, in case you need to borrow one.

The other big item I bought one year was a kitchen cupboard, of the 1950s and 60s style, which I remember from my youth and you might have seen on 'up-cycling' shows, going for around £250. When I told my sensible and practical brother about wanting one of these, he said they were now impossible to find, as everyone wanted them and they were very expensive on eBay.

There was an old tank cupboard built in to the corner of my kitchen, which had become a storage place for kitchen junk. It was full of old saucepans, bags and unused sandwich makers, still covered in immovable cheese and a waste of space. I had cleared it and asked around for someone to help me demolish it, with no luck. I demolished it myself in the end. Mending the ceiling and doing to flooring and redecorating the walls took ages, but I was now ready for my cupboard. A few weeks passed.

There was one at the boot sale, but my heart sank. It stank of something like fertilizer and I guessed it had been in a shed. The two drawers were missing and one leg was rotten at the bottom, but I asked the price anyway. £15. I paid and, as with the ladder, asked for delivery. He agreed, but it didn't arrive.

Later I phoned the chap and he had been trying to call me on my work number, instead of home. We arranged to meet at the Sunday boot sale at Ardleigh, for me to collect it. I wasn't sure how I'd do this, as I was going away on the Saturday and also my car was too small. Ukulele Dave, my best local mate, came to the rescue. He found the chap, got it into his big Volvo estate and took it to his place. Later, he delivered it to me, but he looked sceptical about my ability to do it up. I was too, but had a slow determination.

It was still the summer term at work, so I left it till the break. I managed to make some drawers from old wood; some thick teal shelving for the fronts and ply for the inside. I was surprised that they looked OK. I found the original paint colours, light green and cream, under some badly applied dirty white repaints, and matched them at a paint shop. I mended the back leg and bought some metal discs to raise the legs slightly from the floor. The rest of it was good, including the enamel cold surface that pulls down in the middle. I had bought some fancy but old and funky plastic re-cycled handles, which replaced the top four, the two drawers and the top cupboard with fancy windows. The naff but cool orange and white three that remained went on the middle pull-down and the lower cupboard doors, with the help of a bit of orange plastic and some epoxy. It took me all summer, but it looked great – still does. I took photos and boasted to my brother. A girlfriend said, "Are you coming out, or are you going to stay in and stroke your cupboard?" I replied, "How did you know I stroke it?" If you want bargains, there's one.

I used to find things for my brother Jon. He had a collection of objects in the shape of books and I gave him many over the years. He had lost, or lent, his *Reader's Digest Repair Manual*, so I found him a replacement. He sometimes did a sale himself, as a seller, but would always buy something. From one of these trips, he came back with 20 rungs from an old wooden ladder. They were lovely pieces of worn wood. It was years before he found a use for them.

Eventually they turned into lovely handles for wooden trugs he made. I still have one which I used on my allotment. I should give it away. We both had ladder history. I miss him.

All this thing-ness reminds me that it was just as much about my dear departed friend Ukulele Dave and my own brother, Jon. And about the visions and discussions and life found amid the stalls and the chaos, the bricolage of making a life.

This brings me to my final epigraph, which is from the end of Tennyson's 'The Holy Grail'.

> ...the King must guard
> That which he rules, and is but as the hind
> To whom a space of land is given to plow.
> Who may not wander from this allotted field
> Before his work be done; but, being done
> Lets visions of the night or of the day
> Come, as they will; and many a time they come,
> Until the earth he walks on seems not earth,
> The light that strikes his eyeball is not light,
> The air that smites his forehead is not air
> But vision – yes, his very hand and foot –
> ...
> And knows himself no vision to himself,
> ...
> So spake the King: I knew not all he meant.

The visions of the field: that could be a title of the most

thing-y of boot sale purchases and exchanges. I miss Sarah too, sharer of my visions, and hope she is well and making good art in her fields of vision. We knew not all we meant.

Week 17: FOLK

WEDNESDAY 18TH AUGUST, 2021. MARKS TEY.

Table clip-on mic stand. £4.

Mini violin ornament. £1.

Maglite torch. £3.

Curiosities of Essex. David Occomore. £2.

A Selection. Stevie Smith. 40p.

The Wireless Stars. £1.

An Irish Journey. Sean O'Faolain. 50p.

Sweet Songs of Zion. John Betjeman. 50p.

Talking it Over. Julian Barnes. 50p.

The Corrections. Jonathan Franzen. £1.

FRIDAY 20TH AUGUST, 2021. HORSLEY CROSS.

Strawberries. £1.20.

This week was a musical week and a chatty one. The chaps who sold me the model violin (a gift for my niece), were selling a ukulele, which I tried, tuned and played, making up a parody of 'When I'm Cleaning Windows' that went something like 'When I'm Selling at Boot Sales'. The table clip-on mic stand is a good thing for recording demos, and is already in use. The hymns got me into the thoughts that resulted in Week 15's themes and gave me the title of a home-recorded CD, *Folk Poetry*. I chatted to the people who tried to give me the Stevie Smith poems for free. I insisted on 40p, as I had that in change and told them what my dad used to say: "There's no taste in nothing."

This book has already gone to my pal Jo in Kent, herself a great boot fair person. I also chatted to the posh woman again.

Even at Horsley Cross, buying only strawberries, I advised a woman selling overpriced books on their realistic value. I told her about a nice, two-volume *Shorter Oxford Dictionary* going for £1 on a house clearance stall. I wonder if she bought it. The whole boot sale experience in mid-August is relaxed and friendly.

All this to lead up to my most treasured item of the year, *Curiosities of Essex*, by David Occomore. This is an ex-library book, not yet valuable, and I told the woman selling, after I had paid, that I knew the author. She said I should have told her, as she might have reduced the price. I answered that the opposite might have been true: "...or you might have asked for a tenner!"

When I got the book home, I realised that it was in its essence a ballad-history of Essex – 'Essex History as Seen from Broadside Ballads', as David says in his subtitle. This is a typically brilliant piece of research from David, who I have known since the late 1970s. I read the book straight through and bookmarked a few pages where I liked the ballads, few of which I had seen before. It wasn't much later that I set one to music and performed it in public. Everyone liked it. Since then I have put a traditional-influenced tune to another one from the book.

I think I have all of David's work on Essex now, gathered over the years. It annoys me that nothing of his is still in print and his greatest work of scholarship and musicality had never been published.

When I first started playing in folk clubs, I became a regular singer at the Three Blackbirds club in Leyton High Road. Among the other regulars were the Music Hall quartet Ticklers Jam, one of whose spouses I knew from the past, fiddler Dave Shepherd, later of Blowzabella, Dave Roberts (ditto), and surreal comedian-singer Dave Surman. Alan Bearman, who now runs the Sidmouth Folk Festival, ran this club.

Dave Occomore was another singer. Quiet and unassuming, Dave was at the time, I think, a librarian, though friends tell me he was a postman, with an academic interest in folksong. I chatted to him from my singer-songwriter end of things, but detected a serious and good chap. I think I bought his *Bushes and Briars: An Anthology of Essex Folk Songs* direct from him at the club. The book was created with Philip Spratley and is dated 1979. It is an excellent book and should be in print. I liked what these guys were doing, but it was a long time before I ever felt confident enough to try to sing traditional material. Dave was respectful of what I did and the atmosphere at the club was tolerant, creative and mutually encouraging. We both launched careers from there: him as writer and collector of ballad and songs, history and folklore, and me as a semi-pro club singer-songwriter. Now here was I, excited by what was a new book his, to me, and the potential of the material.

The Curiosities book was produced later, in 1984, as was *Folk Songs Collected in Essex* by Dr Ralph Vaughan Williams, on which he collaborated with Philip Heath-Coleman. This latter, magnum opus, has never been published. Shame on everyone who hasn't published it: Essex County Council, Essex Folk Association, Essex University, EFDSS, the Ralph Vaughan Williams Society, the Vaughan Williams Memorial Library, Essex Libraries – I call you out, I accuse you of neglecting your own culture to your own detriment. Shame on me and on us all who haven't published these 200-plus pages of riches.

I have a photocopy of a photocopy of this book. It is like something forbidden in communist USSR. Come to that why isn't all Dave's stuff in print, if we cared for our own culture?

Dave's last Essex book is *An Essex Pot-Pourri*, mostly folklore and history, but I have a post-it marking a song he includes, which I might yet follow up. This last one dates from 1989 and makes me reflect on how weird it was for folkies in the 1980s. The *Pot-Pourri* ends with a symbolic loaf made for luck and a great storm which happened in 1565. Curses and blessings end things and the 80s never really ended, I sometimes think. Dave gives us some blank pages at the end of the book, to paste in our own collectings, and I feel that maybe I'm doing that here, becoming a folklorist of myself.

The 1980s was a strange time, in retrospect, to start a career in the folk world. The days of 1960s folk revivalism and excitement had passed, the folk-rock days of the 1970s were fading. There was a new spirit in the air, one that favoured money-making and fashion. The 70s were bad enough for the way people dressed but the 80s was worse, not that it affected us. The effect on the folk clubs was a kind of retreat into the niche of our world. Stuff was happening, but it was no longer celebrated in the outside world.

What excited me was the small, mostly London-based music hall revival. Bands like Ticklers and Flowers and Frolics took their cues from pioneers like Bob Davenport, who had always included pop songs and music hall songs among the traditional material. I saw Bob with the Rakes and the variety of music and song they played was exhilarating. I had thought I was on my own with my influences from old 78s and anything English from variety and music hall. It seemed to me that we had a good, honest way ahead. We didn't feel out of the mainstream, either, though we were. Bands that had a punk influence, but remained, like Ian Dury's bands, were doing similar things to us, with a clearly English intelligence. We had an alternative way that still seems viable, to me, now. It went along with the great English Country Dance traditional tune playing of the time.

Even the Englishness of bands like Depeche Mode, who were after all from Essex and lived in the same town as my brother, excited me, though they were of a different generation. I liked the Human League because of Phil Oakey's very English baritone. We were ignored, but, as a songwriter, I liked Pete Coe's description of me as "1980s Music Hall". The world often seemed against us and we were not playing the fame and money game, encouraged by the endless right-swings of the government.

Like David Occomore, I produced my little bit of stuff, my corner of an invisible market. My LP was held up by the record manufacturers producing copies of the charity single, 'Do They Know it's Christmas'. Charity reared its double-edged cold head and hand, with its dubious help and its glory for the great and fund-heavy celebrities. I wrote a song called 'Spare Change' about new beggary and charity. There is a proverb, or expression that says charity is 'cold', and I still think it is. "There's some celebrity / Proud to appeal to me / He thinks he is the cure / But I am ill at ease / And I'm not really sure / He's not part of the disease" – this is from

'Spare Change'.

As well as the LP, I also produced two cassette albums: one a double LP length, called *Hearts and Flyovers*, including my 'Roadworks' suite, and another of a 'one-man musical' *1999½*. People liked my stuff and, although I rarely made a living, I had a career of sorts, not just a roll down a hill, out of control. This time was formative: I was in my thirties and this work, these songs, made me who and what I am.

David Occomore wrote a few other books on different subjects, but he moved away and retired early and now lives far away from his loved and explored Essex. I didn't move away but I moved away from songs being my main focus and ended the 1990s with a PhD and a teaching job at university. Still an outsider, looking at a different inside, one colleague described me as a "refugee from a skiffle group". Although not true, there is some truth in it, somehow.

By the end of the 1980s, the clubs were diminishing in number and many of us, me included, joined various bands, including folk dance bands, to keep going. I joined Spring Chickens, who specialised in witty songs and were often second on the bill at big folk festivals. It was hard to get many festivals as a soloist. I had written lyrics for them before I joined, but enjoyed my time being further up the bill and writing sharp lyrics and gags for the front men, Dave Mitchell and John Spires. I learned masses about arranging and harmony singing. We laughed all the time, it seems to me now, and were safe-wild with our parodies of age and baldness. When they got a bit too showbiz for me, I left on friendly terms, and still wrote lyrics for them.

I sang mostly my own stuff and rarely tried anything traditional, as the singers from that time who performed traditional stuff were so great at it, which made it seem impossible. The wonderful, influential voices of Nic Jones and Martin Carthy, for example, felt intimidating to me. As a fan, I loved traditional song but was convinced that my own stuff justified my existence by being a writer, not a great vocalist. It was much later that I forgave myself for not being good enough to sing traditional stuff and my attention to the strange wonder of it paid off in a little more confidence. I could put a song across, even if I would never be Nic Jones.

Jones' terrible accident in the 1980s feels to me now like a picture of the folk scene. He was the best of us in many ways. The fact that the last of many times I saw him before his road accident featured some brand-new songs seems even more poignant. I suspected, though these new songs sounded traditional, that he had written them. I spoke to him later and asked if they were his own. He seemed pleased that only a songwriter noticed, or commented on it, and I was delighted to think the future held new songs by Nic, now a fellow singer-songwriter. The end of his career came shortly after this occasion. His tragedy was ours.

It was my now friend Sue Cubbin's book of some of Vaughan Williams' collected Essex songs, which pays tribute to Dave Occomore's work, that got me into trying to perform traditional songs. *That Precious Legacy* came out in

2006 and I was asked by my friend Elaine if I could help her perform a couple of the songs at a book event. I ended up in the group called Potiphar's Apprentices, with Sue and her husband John. We are still going. I now have no qualms at trying a traditional song, especially if I can make it my own somehow. Sometimes that means changing the words and often changing the arrangement or the tune.

The work, rooted in past songs, is a nice rest from the inevitable selfhood of being a songwriter-singer and I relish it. This period of plague also turned me back to the traditional material, especially that of my home county. So, the humble singer and nice chap of years ago has become my source. Working on this old stuff is nourishing and feeds all aspects of your writing and immerses you in a different kind of creativity.

It is hard to explain the lure of traditional songs and ballads but, at its best, the stuff has a life and a liveliness, a kind of long-lived common touch that enriches the human condition. The narrative quality is to the fore and this is something I have struggled with in my own writing. At best, the songs can create a world and are emotional as any soul music. Sometimes people complained about songwriters being over-emotional, but folksong is dripping in heartbreak and real pain and is the antidote to the slick happiness of more 'popular' music.

'Warley Camp' is a ballad that caught my attention as soon as I saw it. The barracks at Warley is where the Ford

Motor Company now has a headquarters, and I remember a local older man telling me he trained as an ostler there for the first world war. Rudyard Kipling's son John was also there training, before his early death in the war. This ballad comes from the early days of Warley, when it was just a camp. Dave notes that regiments were sent abroad often "to lessen the urge for desertion" (p15). It makes this song of a poor soldier and his girl seem all the more poignant. It was printed in London and authors are rarely credited, but the writer seems to catch, in the language of folksong, a sense of making a positive from a potential negative. I like this and recognise it. I love the repetition of "handle it and dandle it" for the affection between the potential new parents and their dreams of a family, who will "never let it cry". The themes of soldiering, love among the poor, going abroad and starting a life are all recognisable to us now. A great storm is identified too, so the historical resonance is doubly powerful.

THE NEW WARLEY CAMP
(Military camp at Warley from 1740s; storm 1779)

Farewell my dearest Polly, I am come to take my leave
For I am going to Ireland my pay for to receive
And if you will gang along with me your fortune for to try
Once more we'll go to Warley Camp to lie,
We'll go down to Warley Camp to lie

My daddy and my mammy they swore they would me kill
For keeping soldier's company, but I do love them still

Besides I am with child by you, which thing you can't deny
So along with you to Warley Camp to lie,
We'll go down to Warley Camp to lie

Now if you are with child my love, as I suppose you be
We'll handle it and dandle it, my wife shall follow me
The knapsack for to carry that she will ne'er deny
Once more we'll go to Warley Camp to lie,
We'll go down to Warley Camp to lie

And if it is a female and that perhaps may be
We'll handle it and dandle it and let it on my knee
I'll handle it and dandle it and never let it cry
Once more we'll go to Warley Camp to lie,
We'll go down to Warley Camp to lie

The first place that we arrived at, it was in Warley Park
And there we pitched our tents, me boys, as white as any
          chalk
Until such heavy showers came pouring from the sky
No more we'll go to Warley Camp to lie,
No more go down to Warley Camp to lie

The fourth of December, as I've heard many say
There we struck our tents, me boys, and then march away
With our noble marquees, we hung them out to dry
No more we'll go to Warley Camp to lie,
No more go down to Warley Camp to lie

I did not change much here, except made the short last line into a repeated short chorus, which fits the tune I concocted for it. It is a hopeful song, as well as historical.

The other song I made from Dave's collection is also rooted in history and is a darker story. The story is from 1830 and a time in agriculture of "cold, hunger and unemployment" (p58). There were riots and protests. This ballad seems to try not to take sides, having sympathy for all and mourns the loss of promise in youth. The ballad is untitled and has the real events listed above the verses. I called it 'The Rayleigh Fire, 1830'.

THE RAYLEIGH FIRE, 1830

Oh what a dismal sight of woe and wretched misery
To see so many youths expire upon the fatal tree
What cries and lamentations, what bitter groans we hear
On every side all from their friends and from their kindred
    dear

Ill fated youths, how could you that, all laws divine defy
The precious food that God had sent you basely to destroy
What pleasure could it yield to see the farmer's little store
Consumed by those devouring flames you set at his barn
    door

How often in the dead of night all in the winter's drear
The husbandman lay deep asleep not dreading danger near

Has been aroused all from his bed with sorry heat to see
His stock yard wrapped in flames and be reduced to
	beggary

How many tender mother with bleeding heart may mourn
The loss of her dear son who thus has died a death of scorn
Two blooming youths, two brothers dear, along with
	many more
Have left their broken-hearted friends their downfall to
	deplore

God grant that soon the time may mend and wages may
	increase
And working men with cheerful hearts may spend their
	days in peace
When fractious knaves in fetters bound and branded with
	distain
Shall silenced be then we may see good times return again

Here I did change a few lines to make them fit and make sense, but only by a matter of 10 words in total. The hope and waste of youth are the themes of these two ballads, which are universal themes, still alive in all of us and something we carry through our lives.

I cannot help wondering how much my own and Dave's lives were affected by our coming to creative maturity through difficult times for the folksong-minded. You carry the ability to expect to be misunderstood and underestimated.

But perhaps you gain a degree of nonchalance at the brash nonsense of the world and a certain persistence in your own interests and efforts. I don't know how Dave feels now, as he is far away and not writing about Essex. He was there before me, I guess. If I had any influence, and I don't, I would try and get him an honorary doctorate at my university.

When I got my doctorate, I was delighted that Ronald Blythe, that great local writer and lovely man, got his honorary one in the same ceremony. I have a photo of us both to prove it. Dave's efforts, at a more common folk level, should not be overlooked.

In my classes on lyric writing I always emphasised that many don't listen to the words anyway. The way records are produced these days, with the vocals way back in the mix, is lamentable. A book I bought at the boot sale a few years' back has Flotsam (or B.C. Hilliam) of the variety duo Flotsam and Jetsam, in his autobiography *Flotsam's Follies* (1948) writing a poem to lament this trend. This tendency, I should say, is an eternal problem. His appeal about hearing the words ends his book. His ghost will forgive me for giving it my own title and adding a PS, in brackets.

LYRICIST'S LAMENT

Oh let us hear the words of songs!
  Is it too much to ask
That singers regard the words of songs
  As part of their vocal task?

So often a lovely voice one hears
   With the dulcet charm of a bird's,
But alas one vainly strains one's ears
   To catch one hint of the words,

It was one of our ways in bygone days
   To print the words, so we
Would know what the singer was singing about,
   But today that cannot be.

Therefore a vocalist all the more
   Should make their diction clear
So that the story of their song
   Shall reach our patient ear.

'Down in the forest,' – yes, indeed
   We know that 'something stirred,'
But how can we know what that something was
   If the singer's words aren't heard?

We know 'tis true that writers of verse
   Have suffered much neglect;
The composer's name is the programmed one
   He gets assured respect.

So, singer, the balance rests with you
   To adjust, and so make sure
That the words, by careful clarity,
   Like the music, shall endure.

Alas how vain will have been this plea
    To which I have given tongue,
If I've failed to make you hear the words
    Of the song that I've just sung!

(I'm sad to tell you, Flotsam
    That recent times are worse,
Where wobbly over-singers
    And sound-crews kill your verse)

Week 18: RELIGION

WEDNESDAY 25TH AUGUST 2121. MARKS TEY.

Chapels of Essex. 50p.

Musical Instruments Through the Ages. £2.

On the Abbey of S. Edmund at Bury. M.R. James. £1.

New insoles. £2.

SATURDAY 28TH AUGUST. WEELEY.

Illustrated British Ballads. £1.

Best of Essex Countryside, 1976. £1.50.

There seemed to be very few house clearance stalls this week and I imagined one of them had died and all the clearance people went to the funeral. I imagined it to be very sparse and cleared, dignified, the ultimate clearance. Probably there was a fair nearer London happening. On one stall I saw were boxes full of matchboxes and book-match cases and I imagined my lost boot sale partner taking a picture of them with her phone, as she had with other collections: egg cups, toast racks. There is often something elegiac about boot sales. Life lost as well as liveliness to be found. There was lots of kids' stuff this week, usual in summer and telling of lost childhood, and not too many books I had not already seen in previous sales.

At Weeley, near Clacton, there was a big book stall and I think I recognised the stock, from a secondhand bookshop in Harwich, run by a chap called Peter. His high prices were inside, but they were being sold for £1 a go. More loss, perhaps, this time of a good shop, though I have not been to see if he is still there or not. Maybe just clearing some old stock.

The thing I was most excited to get was the old book on St Edmund's Abbey. This seemed to me to have potential, in value as well as interest. It is dated on the paper cover 1895. *Chapels of Essex* was a good find too, as I had recently written about the 'tin tabernacle' in Old Heath, Colchester, near where I live.

It was towards the end of 2020 that I had followed up my interest in St Edmund. He was a local saint and king, had a strange myth surrounding his death, and I knew he had once been our patron saint. Eventually I bought Francis Young's brilliant book, *Edmund: In Search of England's Lost King* (2018), and became excited, given this was during the pandemic, when I found that he was the patron saint of plagues. His myths and afterlife legends and miracles were various and extraordinary, as if he was the vessel for all our losses. I made a list of subjects and ideas Young's book prompted in me. Most relevant being that the city of Toulouse being saved from the plague was a miracle attributed to him. It was getting towards Christmas, mid-Covid, so I wrote a carol about this. I turned it into a Christmas card, with a photo I found of a painting and the words. The painting had been stolen from a church I had known from childhood, at Greensted, near Ongar. I put the song on my website.

The story of his martyrdom is quickly told. The young king, of early shining promise, was in battle with ruthless invaders, who captured him. They mocked him when he refused to renounce his faith. They tied him to a tree and used him as target practice for their arrows. He was the victim of a jeering, nasty group of invaders. They cut off his head, denying him the integrity of body required by his religion. A wolf calls out, "Here," when his head is sought by his companions and after they find it, it miraculously reunites with his body. His body does not decay, even in the tomb.

Those are the mysterious basic elements of the legend. Thereafter he seems to have the most active life as an inspirer and uniter of the faithful, like an echo of Christ in sacrifice and survival and of youthful promise gone but still alive, though hidden. There is an innocence and oneness with the good and with nature there somehow. He is forgotten, but never somehow gone.

I knew that there was a stained-glass window of St Edmund in my local church, St Leonard's, just a minute from my flat. But you could not get in there, as the church was closed during the plague time. This made me volunteer, later, to become a Friend of St Leonard and do my stint once a month, when the disused church is open for a couple of hours a week. St Edmund and loss was working in me.

ST EDMUND CAROL

Here comes cold December. Crowned King on Christmas
    Day
The scholars say St Edmund's never really been away
You were such a young man, fierce defender, on our side
O curer saint, save England, and the world beside

Sweet St Edmund, England's first patron saint
In our plague, our winter, our fear, under restraint
As you saved the city of Toulouse, return somehow
Our martyr and our warrior King, sweet St Edmund save
    us now

We need more than one saint in chill seasons of disease

When people lose their work, their hope and their families
Defend us like the mother wolf who guards your spirit
    true
You bear our burdens, so hear this carol sung to you

And the carol service won't take place this year
In my local church, but I pick some holly there
There's a stained glass window showing how this martyr
    dies
So I pray, St Edmund, now's the time you will arise

I got to play this carol live, a year later, in December 2021, in St Leonard's and it felt right, finally. The place where St Edmund was reputedly crowned, near Bures, is a lovely little chapel and quite hard to find, on a nice footpath outside the village. I had been there and the setting is lovely. You can see a recently carved chalk dragon from there, reminding me of the medieval dragon at Wiston church, nearby. We got lost finding it. It is just outside Essex, in Suffolk, so not in the chapels book. More loss about loss.

The window in St Leonard's is splendid, by the way, probably made by a commercial firm in the 1920s. I did get to photograph it and now I see it once a month. The 20th of November is St Leonard's feast day and I for one don't see any reason why we should not have two patron saints, as April 23rd and November seem good seasonal times when celebration might be needed. I had also recently written about Burns' night and the need for an English celebration of similar stature: suggesting the name Shakey George Night, as 23rd of April is Shakespeare's birth and death day. This is in my *Tradition in Creative Writing*.

I have a list of ideas from November 2020, stimulated by Young's book, including the idea of the talking wolf guardian of the head and something celebrating his day. The title above the list reads *Songs for St Edmund*. A story of the stolen Greensted painting seemed a good idea too, especially as St Edmund, post-death, had punished thieves at the Abbey.

I couldn't wait to get the book home and look it up. The first thing I noticed was that the author was M.R. James, that most literary of ghost-story writers, which makes the book more collectable. His hauntings are often set in Suffolk and he seems the right man for St Edmund, whose life after death was so huge and various and so haunting. This fact also might make the book really valuable. I could not find a copy for sale. There are reprints, for £20-£30, and you can read the book online for free. Deeper searches reveal a copy had been sold locally at a Colchester auction house, coincidentally. But, at the time, I couldn't find the price. The book seemed closed, as to finding out about it.

Many of the pages were uncut and I was unsure what to do about this. The pages I could see were lists of what used to be in the library, so it looked dry and historical. I took it over to see Bookshop Dave at Stoke-by-Nayland. He didn't rate it and said maybe leave the uncut pages, so I put it aside. Some time later, I went on to the auction house's website and tried to track it down.

I found the estimate in the catalogue: £20-40. Maybe a 'come and buy' temptation. After a long search I found the results – it went for £22. Oh well. I put it aside again. Not worthless and of some interest and still no copies on the internet for sale.

More recently I thought I would like to see the contents properly, so looked up how to cut uncut pages of an old book. The internet helped this time. While I watched a video, I remembered my old book expert Peter Wayland showing me the same technique. It is counter-intuitive. You use an index card or card of similar thickness and not a sharp knife. You angle it obliquely and do it gently. It makes a clean, but not too sharp, and hence not noticeable, cut. Every other page needed doing, so I did them and began reading the book backwards, as the account of the fire of 1465 caught my attention.

James reproduces the Latin document, but then translates it. Young quotes a bit of it in his book (p120), but this is the bit I like:

"Another incident was very surprising, and deserves to be recorded, concerning Egelwyn, the former servant and charioteer of the martyr [this was the monk who had conveyed the body around the country during the Danish terror] and others [e.g. Oswen, the female devotee] whose bones were kept in a wooden chest, high up, near the King's tomb. Some men had employed great force in trying to move them, inasmuch as the heat had already got to them; but, though the chest could ordinarily be lifted with one hand, they were now unable to stir it. Was not this truly a faithful servant, who refused to forsake the King?" (p211).

This great fire, from which St Edmund's shrine was left intact, was started by the accident of some plumbers' brazier. "Some of the utensils of divine service" were stolen, "removed by unprincipled persons" (p208). The fire starting, the theft and the miraculous saving of the shrine and servants all speak of the difficulty of the survival of any sense of power and the sacred, as if it were our own time. St Edmund is still subject to thefts and arrows piercing him anew, you might say.

James's introduction to part one of the book talks of the abbey having "a whole body of men who in their time were a mighty power in Eastern England, nay, at the ruling centre of England itself" (p1). Very few know the story of St Edmund, even so, despite the inspired efforts of Francis Young. There had, previous to 1465, been riots and another fire that threatened the Abbey Church. "Unprincipled persons" with no sense of the sacred are always around and the appeal of the martyr has faded into an obscure part of unlikely history, or legend, still hidden and uncut, like my obscurely valuable book.

As Young says, "St Edmund has historically been a unifying rather than a dividing symbol... veneration for Edmund's memory united English and Dane, and Norman and even

Catholic and Protestant at the time of the Reformation." He was "the guarantor of a composite national identity for the English". He can be seen as "denying any attempts to reduce Englishness to any facile ethnic nationalism" (p155).

I want to go and research the painting stolen from Greensted-juxta-Ongar, as it seems to me indicative of his continued martyrdom, of everything taken, including early life, in the cruellest way – and yet some good, some sacredness remaining, however hidden away. I still feel there are stories and lines to talk about him, which I need to find. What would the wolf say? The confrontation of goodness and innocence with a brutal, literal world seems written through his stories, right up to now, and they continue, as his grave is still sought. I saw Francis Young talking about this, in a clip from local TV, on his website. Saint Ed is lost and still affirming his liveliness in martyrdom.

I visited some of the St Edmund churches in Essex in the summer of 2020, though most of them were closed. Still, I expect they do not have much of the saint in them. Any church is a nice place to visit, even merely outside. East Mersea is especially pleasing, where Sabine Baring-Gould was vicar, who collected folksong and wrote his novel *Mehalah* about the island. There is a good bit about him in the *Essex Countryside* compilation book bought at Weeley, dated January 1968. There is a caged grave of a teenage girl there at East Mersea church, who might have been a Mehalah, who was a rebel.

Now, the closed churches and hidden book tell me a different story. The M.R. James was hidden in the bottom of a grubby box, along with the big musical instrument book. The latter has some great pictures of obscure instruments and some good old medieval paintings in it. I pressed it in my book press, as it was a bit wrung, as we say in the book world. M.R. James' name was given in full on the cover of the Abbey book, so I did not recognise it until I looked it up. The pages were hidden by being uncut and the value is still hidden. Where is St Edmund? Hidden, lost, mourned by a faithful few, like his servants who would not be moved.

Since writing my collection of poems and songs *Discovering England* (2017) is has occurred to me, from reading strangers' accounts of us, that they notice our lost and fallen nature more than we do. 'The Empire's Decline' sounds like a title, or the name of a cinema or music hall, but I am convinced that the great song of loss that is England is an unconscious thing to us, by and large. We have been falling down for so long that it looks normal; it looks like stability. When will we hit the bottom? If you see the current government as part of the long decline, that is the only way they make any sense. Until it stops, our decline is what I notice, with its backward-looking, regretful, xenophobic contortions and its failure to be alive to the sacred and the positive. If you listen closely, you can hear the decline, the great sob of loss. It is not the end of the world, but you can see it from here.

St Edmund has become my emblem for this – and my hope. It was a sunny day, early in the year, with a gentle breeze, when the great fire of 1465 started. It was a sunny day in the same early part of the year that I visited the site of the old abbey, just a few days ago as I write, to add something to this meditation on St Edmund.

Going out anywhere at this moment in plague-time still seems unusual and a bit scary. Arriving in a big town car-park has an alienating effect. I drove into one, having no idea if I was anywhere near the abbey. I remember people being killed in car-parks in movies and TV crime dramas. I approach the machine; the only welcome. It has a baffling message that a tall woman is trying in vain to decipher. She asks me, in a strong Suffolk accent, what it means. I have no idea, but I ask her about the abbey gardens. She directs me towards them and I drive away.

I meet my old, dear friend, who lives in Suffolk, and we go to the cathedral, which is not dedicated to Edmund, to find the café and have lunch. The tourist centre and shop are closed but they have a few items of tourist-ware for sale. I find the only booklet on the Saint and try to buy it. It is an overpriced £4. I could easily have stolen it, as no-one seemed to look at any of the stuff in a small display. I take it to the café checkout and they don't know what to do. The cashier has to consult someone else. They take my money but do not enter it into the till. The saint is hidden and overlooked. His one presence sold almost reluctantly and unofficially. I am amused, as the saint's absence becomes more palpable.

The ruins of the church are like a lunar landscape of waste and decay. They look alien and stalagmite-like. It is another planet, when St Edmund was there. We wander around a bit, but there is little information about the abbey. We find a garden shop which has a bit of tourist-ware and I buy a fridge magnet of a wolf guarding a crown and one of a sculpture of a vague figure which might be him. The 20-page pricey booklet is good, even though the pictures are not listed or acknowledged. It has a useful map. I notice that the catholic church is dedicated to St Edmund and ask my friend to take us there, as she knows the town.

Here, by contrast, St Edmund is very visible and in our visit to the town, only here. The building is lovely too, a Victorian-looking, corn-exchange atmosphered big space with lightness and calm all through. Around the walls are panels and big, recent tapestries of the Saint's story, made by schoolchildren. These are there in the booklet too, though uncredited. There is a statue of the saint which we photograph. At last, I feel I have arrived with the presence of the saint, away from the great fugue of loss and decline.

The catholic church's 'St Edmund's News' is putting on some events for '1,000 years of the Abbey of St Edmund'. There is a talk about St Edmund called 'Where does the truth lie?' I wonder if the chap doing it embraces the ambiguity? I wonder if he sees the metaphor of fall, of decline, of loss of England? They also had a guided tour, called 'Edmund – a pilgrim's view', which sounds good, but had already happened.

It was a good feeling to know I had arrived in a place which embraced the hidden Saint and feel myself blessed. I had a bit of sunburn on my cheeks from the day, but found my pilgrimage satisfactory at least, and at last, here.

We took a photo of me by the tennis courts in the gardens, as I remembered that Francis Young, among others, says St Edmund might be buried under there, but later I read that they had moved the courts anyway. I cannot find an update on the search for his remains, which seems fitting, nor still a value for my old book. No-one was playing tennis, and there was a warning about abusive language being used by players. We are 'unprincipled persons', all. So, I don't know where he is, or where he might be, our old king, our patron saint of loss and lostness, easy to find but hard to see.

A Book of Magicians edited by R...

Roger Lan...

Roger Lancelyn Green: Tales of Ancient Egypt

Roger Lancelyn Green: Tales of the Greek Heroes

The Tale of Troy

Roger Lancelyn Green: Myths of the Norsemen

THE ANATOMY OF MELANCHOLY I BURTON

THE ANATOMY OF MELANCHOLY II BURTON

BOHN'S POPULAR

BOHN'S POPULAR

Week 19: RICHARD CHURCH

WEDNESDAY 1ST SEPTEMBER. MARKS TEY.

Soup bowl, Royal Cauldon. £1.

Kent (The County Books). Richard Church. £1.

The Black Book. Lawrence Durrell. £1.

SATURDAY 4TH SEPTEMBER. BRAINTREE.

White undercoat paint. 50p.

Disgusting Bliss: The Brass Eye of Chris Morris.

Lucian Randall. 50p.

Once you step out of the mainstream, out of the subtle dictatorship of it, life opens us in gentle and unexpected ways. You can then come across the strange items outside your radar and find something new or forgotten and widen your vision. Boot sales have this feel about them. The quiet and ordinary speculators seek to be taken out of themselves into a small passion.

Three or four years' back, at Marks Tey, I came across a book by Richard Church (1893-1972). It was a book of essays, a signed first edition of *Calm October* (1961). It became my book of the year and I ended up buying and finding his poems and works of autobiography. His work is quiet, often nature based, thoughtful, unflashy and full of gentle wit and insight. I own six books by him and have waited until now to find an excuse to write about him.

I tend to like writers who are essayists and those who write in more than one genre. Examples might be Margaret Atwood, D.H. Lawrence and Thomas Hardy. Priestley I have already discussed. Eliot and Auden were great essayists in the days before such things became unfashionable. Is fashion turning round? Church is a good psychogeographer. As a creative writing tutor, I was keen to see what writer/ critics said about the world and about writing, as a more heartfelt, informed version of true literary criticism. I grew to hate 'theory' and read Auden's *The Dyer's Hand* instead. These helped me in my own commentary work for my PhD. I am still writing in this liberated style.

Calm October starts with an essay on the essay, I noticed, after seeing Church's small, neat signature on the title page. This I liked too, as I did a class on just that with my creative non-fiction group. Zadie Smith on the essay is brilliant – she loves its creativity and her own essays are great. Church points out how people used to buy books of sermons and how Tennyson, for example, sold loads of books in his lifetime. He hopes essays are coming back. This seems not to be true until recently. The deserts of the theorised 1980s and 90s were looming over the horizon and the gentler Church would be deserted. He could make a comeback now, though. A selected works would be good, with poems and prose. I volunteer to edit it.

My students used to be amazed that they could be free in essay writing, as they had the drudge of essays as a kind of ritual punishment drilled into them. Academic essays are a drudge and lead to the endless repetition of clichés, like "in this essay", before pointless pre-capitulation of the dull, stock answers. The literary essay came to some of my students as a revelation and liberation. "Don't use the phrase in this essay,'" I told them. "I know its an effing essay, I've seen one before!" Except I didn't say "effing".

"Humility is always acceptable, for it is the pointer to faith in something: and where there is faith, there is likely to be vigour of mind," Church says, with the characteristic good nature of his open attitude. You feel you are in good company, and you are.

He is good on other writers. It's hard to get a copy of John Stewart Collis's *The Triumph of the Tree* for less than £20 now, but there is a small book by him among the *English Journeys* box set I bought earlier this season (Week 3), called *The Wood*, which is extracted from his famous *The Worm Forgives the Plough*. "Mr Collis has contrived, by some remarkable touch of poetic skill, to make us see the forests of the world," he says (p80). I wish someone would review me as 'Dr May'. I imagine now even police arresting you would call you by your first name. There's a lovely appreciation of the later poetry of Sassoon I have bookmarked and an essay on 'Public Occasions', where he lets himself become at one with a crowd, feeling free like one might do at a boot sale.

Anyway, the Wednesday yielded his book on Kent. He obviously loved his adopted county. The county books series are always worth getting, also from that era when these writer types could show their appreciation and literary feelings with a fold-out map and many quotations. This reminds me that the abbey book from last week also has a fold-out map. Just as Kent has Canterbury, its most holy place, so East Anglia has Bury St Edmunds.

I was delighted to get the book for its own sake but also as it gave me my excuse to reread and discuss Church himself. Chapter 15, 'The Belated Pilgrim' allows him to approach faith again, with caution, as I have tried to do in my thoughts about St Edmund. "The Christ-idea persists, or we must perish. This century sees us fighting for it desperately against the forces of economics which are tending to degrade us into an antlike way of life, that permits no individual mystery." Here comes the internet! "We go to Canterbury by a more roundabout way..."

Pilgrimage was a big thing once. I am reminded here of the wonderful Powell and Pressburger film *A Canterbury Tale* (1944) from the same decade as *Kent* (1949) and its strange, roundabout pilgrim and war themes.

Both these mention The Pilgrim's Way, about which Belloc wrote a book, *The Old Road* (1904). I think I have a copy of the latter from an earlier year of boot sales. Like all the best writers, Church makes you want to read more. His book bristles with useful quotations and you feel that postwar optimism informed writers like him. I like to share this feeling, now largely a curious relic of good, hopeful, fair communality.

Collis's and Belloc's work, and checking the Talking Pictures website for the Powell and Pressburger film, are filling up my desk. My own memories of Kent come back and I am in a small folk club in the busy Medway towns, then in a small one in the narrow lanes further south. I played at a club associated with the Loose Women dance team, from Loose, near Maidstone, back in the 1980s.

Church says he has "no excuse for writing" yet another book about Kent, except for reasons of love. "Poets still come here, seeking more than they know," he says, on the final page. I like Kent, but I always used to point out how they took money on the Kent side of the Dartford Crossing, not on my Essex side.

If you look on the internet for poems by Church, you

might find 'The Seal', possibly under a changed title, like 'Concrete'. This is a good poem about endless new building and the natural world in the presence of a pigeon. See also, you might say, the song 'Build' by the Beautiful South. The poem gets used I think, by schools.

Another classic sometimes remembered is 'Mud', about the trenches of the First World War. This is a ritual-sounding poem of the ruin of man in nature again, as all is "trodden into slime". This would be a good song or sound good chanted aloud.

'Two Ways' is something that gets used in funerals and memorials, as it is about death. Somewhere between the fear and the 'friend', as Stevie Smith puts it, is Church's view: "... Death, our neighbour," as he says, at last, "Perhaps it is not too much, / After life's labour." This is a short poem, but worth finding.

Many of his other poems are of seasons and gardening and I love the small scale of his work. There are many memorable lines. 'The Wych-elm' is a lovely poem of a familiar tree, "an old neighbour," echoing the above poem. 'Home from the Woods', which follows this in *Collected Poems* (1948), is also great: "Strange to be home from the woods. / The streets are brittle and hard.' On a similar line, 'The Tree Gazer' is a favourite: lying on his back, he says, "I look up into green wells."

Church continued publishing poems until 1967 and was, in the main, an old-fashioned good poet, without pretensions. He had his say on poetry in his bestselling autobiography, *Over the Bridge* (1953) about calling and simplicity. 'Simplicity' is also the title of another good poem. He mentions "a reverence for tradition and an avoidance of eccentricity" and goes on to assert "the belief that poetry, and indeed all art, should in its first purpose be a communication, as direct and simple as possible". When I read this, I was cheering. He knows that this "has made my work uninteresting to experimentalists, and those critics who have fostered the fashion for puerilism and obscurity in the arts... The aim of simplicity and complete candour in poetry is dangerous because it is so proudly ambitious" (p227). Puerilism is a kind of wilful childishness, which I notice so much in songwriting, as well as singing. And yes, it is ambitious to be simple. These, the subtleties of simplicity, are not in fashion, where such old verities are overlooked as being too obvious or subtle for the up-to-date. For me, his stuff has lasted because of its simple virtues, which I also aspire to. His poems are again not in print at present.

I hope he would have liked my Week 15 defence of 'bad' poetry, even in his quality. On the same page he says, "A writer's life is not solemn. It is a release... an extravagant claim, even a wantonness."

Church and Collis remind me of my dad. Collis's most famous work is about farm-work during the second war. My Dad did the same thing and also wrote about farming for *Farmers' Weekly* and elsewhere. Dad's farm job came about by living in an old farmhouse, and because all the journals, which had been his living, closed during the war –

organically, you might say. On the other hand, Collis's farm job was deliberately chosen. Dad might have written his reminiscences of that time, but he was always looking to the future and writing new things, though his own poems looked back to learning to plough, for example. These men were of a genre of intellectual workers on the land, who wrote books and poems after world wars. I have read quite a few of these men and tend to buy them for my friend Professor Lisa Jack, who specialises in agricultural accountancy. I make a mental note to talk to her about John Stewart Collis.

Browsing the *Kent* book again, I come across Otford. I used to take a detour through that pretty village, before the M25 was finished, on my way across to gigs in Kent or Sussex. There was a big second-hand shop in the centre and in 1981 I bought Priestley's Lost Empires there, along with Fairport Convention's single 'Meet on the Ledge', I remember.

I had learned that the chap selling things did not like selling anything at all. Some are like this, even at boot sales. They are a breed. After a couple of visits, I found the best way was to bring him the item you wanted and offer a specific cash sum. I bought an old knitting machine case to use for an electric guitar, for £1, by this cash-in-hand method. There are so few of these kinds of shops now, but the boot sale helps.

Lost Empires is a classic about the music hall and a darker version of *The Good Companions*, which is still a wonderful book of Priestley's about community and the stage, and he likewise championed simplicity, as we have seen. The Fairport single is also a pioneering work of wonder at the industry of 'making songs', to quote the sublime Richard Thompson's lyrics. There I am, on the road and buying words and music about the very thing I was doing. I do not think the old second-hand place is there still, with its comically reluctant salesman. I checked a few years later.

The Chris Morris biography tells a darker side of creative showbiz, where the subject battles with his media bosses and challenges them. I notice now that he has moved into films and rarely appears in person. He started life, I learn for the book, as a musician from Colchester, and I wonder if he ever aspires to simplicity.

One of my happiest folk club memories comes from Kent in the 1980s, in a regular gig at Broadstairs Folk Club. It is a long journey, passing another great folk club town, Faversham, on the way. But the gigs were good. A few years after the event, a man wrote to me who had seen me at the club. He wanted to buy a copy of my LP *Anarchy in the Ukelele*. He had been on a first date and the couple had come to the folk club, taking pot luck in seeing a guest they had never seen before. It was me.

When I sent the LP, I enclosed a note congratulating them on their forthcoming wedding. He had bought the album as a gift for his new wife in memory of their first date. "It's a wonder I didn't put you off!" I remember writing. What a nice thing to have happened. The nearest to that was a barn dance band gig for a wedding, which had been particularly good, musically. I later met the married couple – 25 years after the event – and they remembered it as a great night too. These little magic things do happen.

Setting off to Kent, which is very near, always felt like going to a very different place, far away. Crossing the Thames is still a larger event than miles. It had the energy of elsewhere and I remember sitting in a layby which had a coffee stall and view of a river, near Otford, often. I was on my way. My first radio broadcast was on BBC Medway. I managed to tune in with a long aerial, from my dad's in south Essex. A small, proud moment.

My humble career in folk clubs sends me back to Church's second volume of autobiography, which covers his growth as a poet, *The Golden Sovereign* (1957). He writes again about simplicity, which "began to attract me as the highest aim of all artists". He elaborates on this: "I would make it my purpose to write poems deceptively simple, in which the depth and universality of feeling and thought would be almost naively expressed, as in folk-song, and therefore diamond-hard, as unforgettable as the form was unfashionable." This he calls "a formidable task... I was veering away from the artistic tendencies of the age, the revolt against tradition and historical roots, which were to dominate..."(p174-5). His meaningful stance against the mainstream pays off still, I believe, as it did for me, in my small way. Later, he recalls his polite friendship with T.S. Eliot, who had reservations about Church's stuff, but who did actually publish one volume of "experiments" (p234), *Mood Without Measure* (Faber, 1927).

I like the last sentence of this second autobiography, which reminds me in cold February, as I write of last September, of the old boot sale. "Still I remain suspended in wonder at the mysterious identity between death and birth, and I have not yet put down my pen."

Charity shops, I know, chuck away a lot of old hardbacks from the 1950s, but I beg them to save any Richard Church volumes. Press them on unsuspecting literary types, I suggest. Boot sales with their indiscriminate salvage, their savage salvage, are the place. This week was jolly and had a late-term feel. Some Royal Cauldon plates go for more than £100 on the internet. My greenish one is delicious, good for soup or cereal. People were chatty, including a man who was desperate to talk music, or "muso" with me, to the point of neglecting his customers. He remembered Friedman's store in Leytonstone, as did I. I considered buying a 1970s version of the Tao, but on reading one or two of the verses, decided not to; a bit too 70s and there were better versions from the 60s, one of which I already own, probably bought here also. Both sales were relaxed and enhancing, with small, happy purchases.

Thinking of these lost empires of words and folk-poetry reminds me that my other bought author of the week, Lawrence Durrell, was an interesting poet too, though it's not been my luck to find his verse at a boot sale yet. Richard Church was prolific, so his work is around. Recently I have frequently seen the first two volumes of his autobiography, but none so far of his novels or later books of poems, or other volumes of essays, but I am on the lookout. And I will be again in a few weeks. The simple, subtle, savage salvage of gentle insight inspires me.

Week 20: HARMONICAS

WEDNESDAY 8TH SEPTEMBER, 2021. MARKS TEY.
One-egg-wonder frying pan (new). £3.
Blues Harp and Marine Band. Alan Blackie Schackner.
£1.50.

**FRIDAY 10TH SEPTEMBER, 2021. HORSLEY
CROSS.**
The Dragon Empress. Marina Warner.
John Piper (Penguin Modern Painters).
Aubrey Beardsley. Brian Reade, V&A.
Robert Louis Stevenson. Bryan Bevan.
The Testament of Mary. Colm Tóibín. (5 for £1.)
Tiny ring binder. £1.
Primer paint. 50p.
Strawberries. £1.20.

I bought the harmonica book in the hope there might be some mention of the humble harmonica harness, holder or rack. No mention at all. I have another harmonica book, *The Natural Blues and Country Western Harmonica* by Jon Gindick. No mention there, either. But I will not be dissuaded. I am obsessed with this necklace of music, this brace of the wails, this one-man-band device, this iron collar of folky love and bluesy lore. I'm exaggerating, but still.

There is a curious parallel with the one-egg-wonder frying pan, which was a real bargain – they normally go for a tenner at least. It is the one-man-band thing in food form: faintly comic but very useful and self-reliant. Boot sales are full of people like that but I have never seen a harmonica harness on a boot sale stall. There is a reason for that. They have an inbuilt stress-point which tends to make them become useless and also careful, one-man-wonder persons keep them and mend them somehow.

The history of the harmonica harness runs parallel with that of the harmonica, of course. The harmonica, possibly invented way back in China, was reinvented by the rise of free-reed instruments in the early 19th century and quickly became an instrument of the people. The earliest image of a rack, harness or holder I can find is from c.1865 and is a homemade wooden neck-worn suspended shelf kind of thing.

Carson Robison used a modern metal one in the 1940s. Earnest 'Pop' Stoneman, in the 1920s, had a spindle of harmonicas in several keys and Jessie Fuller had a whole one-man-band outfit a bit later, in the 1950s and 60s. His 'San Francisco Bay Blues' was a must for early folk/blues players in England.

I saw the US songwriter John D. Loudermilk, who wrote 'Abeline' and 'Tobacco Road' among many other hits, in the Harlow Playhouse Theatre in the 1970s. He featured a guitar-mounted rack arrangement of his own device and impersonated a car changing gear on his 'Road Hog' song. I later stole this effect for my 'English Driving Blues'. I have searched on the internet for his very minimal but effective one-armed clamp but there is no mention of this device on any website, including the one dedicated to him. The harmonica rack is the neglected one again.

One man who pays it proper respect is the great Bob. Bob Dylan is responsible for the revival of the harp-rack in the 1960s. His *Chronicles: Volume One* (2004) is a great book on the "growth of a poet's mind", in Wordsworth's phrase, and he pays respect to the harness that helped him. He records finding a harness in a dusty basement corner of a music shop, obviously unsold from years ago, which he buys. Music shops used to be like that. This was early on in his career, before he had left the Minneapolis folk scene. It was "probably the only harmonica rack at the time in the Midwest. Racks were impossible to find. I'd used a lopsided coat hanger for a while, but it only had sort of worked. The real harmonica rack that I found was in the basement of a music store on Hennipen Avenue, still in a box unopened from 1948." This is from chapter five, p256-7.

It is going to be impossible not to talk about harmonicas too, so I should say that my first instrument was a harmonica, an Echo Super Vamper, the English version of the Marine Band, bought for, I think, 8s 6d, which is about 32½ pence. The *Melody Maker* told you which one the blues and folk musicians played and this was it. I used to go and sit in the big playing field at school by myself and compose Dylan-like songs, complete with harmonica solos. No guitar at that stage, but it was inevitable already that the day would come when I would need a harmonica holder. I was 14.

Aged about 18 or 19, I got the 339 bus from Bovinger Mill to Brentwood and went down the arcade. This was behind where Specsavers is now. Why anyone closed arcades of shops I will never know. These places are romantic, even magic. Right down the far end of this one was the small shop Bandbox, which lived up to its name. They seemed to have everything: records, guitars, trumpets, accessories and harmonica harnesses. It was important to me that I got one like Bob's, small and neat. It was maybe 10s, about 50p. Many of these great shops used to be run by old dance band musos, who had been around and had sympathetic feelings for their customers. I loved Bandbox and I think I bought Syd Barrett's first solo LP *The Madcap Laughs* there, later on.

This harness served me well for years, even when, as with English Driving Blues, I only used it once in a night's gig. The bit that wears out is the adjustment butterfly or wing nuts and the bolts where the harness pivots to adjust it to the right distance from your mouth. Over the years, mine had many changes of these, where the threads became worn. Visits to DIY stores were frequent and I still have tins with butterfly nuts and thin bolts awaiting the readjustment. I still have this harness and I still like the one-man-band feel of an instrument played with hands and the mouth-harp over the top.

At times I have used one with a kazoo in, or a kazoo and harmonica both, like Don Partridge did in his number one, one-man-band hit 'Rosie'. Les Barker, comic poet, even used to sport a slice of malt loaf for a mid poem snack in his. Any comic Dylan, protest singer act needs one to take the mick. In the Burch Brothers' Band, Malcolm used to call it my 'Plastic Donovan Outfit'. Unfair to Donovan, who only used one early on, I think, and wrote some good songs too. You have to put up with a little mockery if you make the solo stand of multi-instrumental individuality. My affection for my harness never wavered, even when I didn't use it. It used to travel in my melodeon case or duffle bag, and now in the pocket of my soft guitar case.

Having a harmonica was useful in the early days before tuners and the pitch pipe is a type of harmonica too. They were around but harmonica harnesses were still a bit unusual, but special for that reason.

The first public performance I ever gave was at the Queen's Head, Churchgate Street, Old Harlow, at Harlow Folk Club. Cliff and I had three songs, just enough for a floor spot. One I had written featured the harmonica. Cliff had written one too. The third was half written by Cliff, then I added words to finish it off. When I think back, they were kind to us and we went down well and felt encouraged. I got my harness a bit tangled in my long hair. From these sparse years, that now looks laughable. These days my white beard is a more likely hazard, or my glasses.

Cliff and I also used the harnesses for kazoos, where we did a jazzy break in a comic song. We stole an introduction to the kazoos by saying his was an alto and mine a baritone, which was nonsense but funny. There was an album out at the time called something like *The Thousand Guitars of Bert Weedon* (or another player like him). We always joked that our album might be called *The Thousand Kazoos of Clifton Prior*. Cliff was later in the comedy group Baby Grand. He wrote a guitar instrumental, in fact, and called it 'I Can't Play the Piano Either'.

The harness was also used in blues-based bands I was in later. An added harmonica always gave a bit extra to a song. There were always lots of jokes about harmonicas, as well as a few about harnesses. Lee Brilleaux said in interview that he always used a triple vodka to wash his harmonicas. When the interviewer asked him if that wasn't rather expensive, he said, "No – I drink it afterwards." This was only one cut above the chap I saw who joked about finding a takeaway meal in his harmonica.

I remember seeing a singer and guitarist who had a harness do a spot in a London folk club. He did three songs and not once was the harmonica in the same key as the song. Somehow, he managed to play, in two different keys, through each solo. It would have felt rude to explain, but I was in awe in a way, as it seemed quite a feat, even if unintentional.

These days I use harmonica occasionally in the traditional folk group I play with, and often for recording. I collect old harmonicas and always check out new harness types. I notice at the moment that Dunlop have one with an extra, single arm, which has the holder on the end. It does look more adjustable and I am tempted to try one. You can get ones from Hohner that look normal but cost about £70. There was a clamped one that fitted onto a guitar, made in Hungary, but it now seems no longer available for sale. There is a good clip on the internet of someone using one, though. Mic-stand holders seem to be about $100 and only available in the USA. I have a plan to convert an old metal music stand into a harmonica clamp-stand with a couple of bolts and wing-nuts and a piece of aluminium carpet holder. I'll let you know how it goes.

My pal John has promised to look into the John D. Loudermilk device and see if he can make one for me, but I won't expect it unless he has time. Meanwhile I bought a bigger one, my second, so that a bigger harmonica could be accommodated, but mainly as my big glasses stop me easily putting on my narrower, original one. This recent one is a Stagg, just from my local music store. Only my second in a lifetime, not counting the bolts and wingnuts. Can I get some with hardened steel? Maybe a blacksmith. I idly wonder about suspending a holder from my glasses, but realise I am getting silly. What do you mean, getting?

I notice that the Wikipedia page only has a few lines about the variable quality of harmonica holders and suggests you try them out before you fix on one that works. The necklace effect is always potentially comic and dangerous but I like to have one about for special song occasions.

Harmonica harnesses will never be cool, despite Dylan's exceptional talent and style. John D. Loudermilk came to the UK in the 1980s and did a TV series for the BBC and you can see clearly his unusual holder, which seems to work fine, attached to the strap button at the neck end of the guitar somehow. I haven't told John about my plan with the music stand, in case it doesn't work.

A holder of Dylan's, used on the Grateful Dead tour, went for £2,700 at Sotheby's. There is much disagreement about Dylan's harmonica playing on the internet. People say, how come he was good on the harmonica at first, then became bad. Personally, I love to hear him play and feel that his harmonica fits with his words and that any album that has a bit on is better, as it is his roots showing. The solo on 'You're a Big Girl Now', from *Blood on the Tracks* is great and expressive. It is part of him and those who don't get his traditional roots, certainly are not going to get the harmonica, let alone the harness of the travelling one-man vibe of his whole thing.

As well as working on my stand-holder arrangement device, I am starting work on a song or poem about the harmonica harness. So far I have one line, possibly the title, 'My Harmonica's Out of Reach'. Here I hope to tap into the inherent comedy of not setting your wing-nuts tight enough, so the harmonica always stays the same impossible distance from your mouth. We'll see how it goes, but it could take a while. There are many ways you can get it wrong. Wrong key, harp the wrong way round, limp wing-nuts, pinging out of the spring holder, getting your tie caught, getting it caught on something backstage or on stage, or getting to the stage. It will take some crafting to make a lyric work, but it could be the only song ever written about the humble rack, harness or holder. A few rhymes there, surely?

A friend has reminded me that the great Sid Kipper used to do a bit of comic business with trying to reach a suspended instrument, but he does owe me a song. I once told him a joke that had been going round the pub music scene in East Anglia. This is how it went: There was a duo called Norfolk and Good (say it out loud), who later changed their name to Suffolk and Watt (ditto). He took the first part of this and, the Kipper Family being Norfolk, called a song by that title: "We are the boys who are Norfolk and good". I miss Sid, as he has retired, mostly. He did buy me a pint for that one, by the way. A naturally very witty and brilliant man, both as Sid and as himself.

Since writing the above, I found my 1960s harness and looked at it under my magnifying lamp (boot sale, £5). It was made by 'Elton, Pat July 1967, No 3332310'. A quick look for Elton harmonica holders on the internet revealed that there is one in the Smithsonian Museum in the USA and they seem to have the original patent, dated 1929. It is likely Bob's first rack, as he calls them, is from the same source. The reason I liked my one was that it looked like his.

I looked up ones for sale and found something interesting. eBay had one, an Elton, in its original box. Just like Bob Dylan finding one from 1948, 'unopened'. The box is white with a simple line drawing of a man using a holder on the front. I seem to recognise it and I am sure my holder came in a similar box. Looking more closely, I realised that it was a guitar-mounted one that was offered for sale, for $30, plus $8 postage. Wow, that is rare and just what I want.

I messaged the seller to ask if he would ship to the UK, but he declined. Unsure what to do, but keen to get the thing, I thought of my poet pal Adam Neikirk. I knew he was going to visit home in the States soon. I emailed him.

He quickly replied. He was in fact already at home in the USA! Even better. Adam comes from a songwriting father and a songwriting grandfather and is a good one himself. He understands folk apparatus. He has bought it for me and will bring it with him when he returns to Essex at the end of the month. I am ridiculously excited.

Here is a rough draft of the song. All this from one book which fails to mention the holder at all. I do believe there is no other song about harmonica holders – a world first.

MY HARMONICA RACK OR HOLDER

My harmonica's out of reach
Can't make a squeak, a wail or screech
I move my mouth forward and back
But I can't get nearer to my harp rack
Need to play that solo before I get older
With my harmonica rack or holder

Why did I harness myself thus
With this my groovy harmonica truss
The rest of the band must hate my guts
But they don't know about worn out wing-nuts
My blushes aren't cool, they're a fiery furnace
When I can't get near my harmonica harness
Chorus

Real cool players say What the heck
Don't need nothing wrapped round my neck
Jagger: Paul Jones, that 60s face
Were not encumbered with a neck brace
They were hip, out of my league
They didn't suffer from metal fatigue
Chorus

If you want to stay cool and stay in the loop
You don't want to suffer from on-stage droop
This dilemma is not so nice

To find you're hoist by your own device
Halfway to paradise is where I stay
When I play so near, yet so far away
Chorus

I look dumb, like Peter Framp
-ton with his tube, with my harp clamp
I just can't make my mouth organ squawk
It's a fault of adjustment, a matter of torque
Thought I was versatile and couldn't fail
But I'm chasing my harp like a dog its tail
Chorus

I already have a tune and a plan for performing. In intend to wear a rack, deliberately set wrong, then at the end, as if in frustration at trying and failing to play a break between every verse, I finally, at the end, rip the harp from the rack and play an unaccompanied solo!

This may also be the only monograph in existence about the subject and I am proud of elevating such a humble thing to the status of a whole chapter, not to mention a song. I am tempted to buy the Hohner posh one as a reward but that would challenge the humility of the thing. When Adam gets back with my rack we shall have a song swap with my holder on my back. He says they have plenty of racks lying around at home. A one-egg wonder and a one-man band / Where the boot sale leads you cannot be planned.

Week 21: FAIRYTALE ENDINGS

FRIDAY 17TH SEPTEMBER 2021.
HORSLEY CROSS.

Old notebook with narrow lines. 20p.

80 Fairy Tales. Hans Christian Andersen. 50p.

Man and the Spiritual World. Arthur Chambers. 50p.

Munich. Robert Harris. 50p.

Strawberries. £1.20.

It is the last boot sale of the year at Horsley Cross and everyone is keen to sell but there's not much new stock around. The old notebook I am already using, as seen in Week 14. But the slip-cased – Hans Christian Andersen book, from the Anderson Museum in Odense, Denmark, is a nicely rounded book to end with. It has the boxed and magical motif of Week 1 (and elsewhere), plus fairytales have that clichéd happy ending. Well, of course, not all of them do.

The Andersen looks to me like it was bought in the gift shop of the museum. It is a bit over-produced. It has a thick box with an ugly photo of the author, and the book inside is heavily bound with quality paper but, oddly for the English-reading tourist, features Danish-style quotation marks, which look like this: >> ... <<. Nonetheless, it is larger and more recent than my old Oxford edition of Andersen.

In relation to other collectors and adaptors of fairytale in his time, Andersen stands out as a creative soul. He does not easily fit, except as a traditional creative, like Burns, who, though immersed in his native culture, added much to it himself in the kind of interactive way I like. Despite the conventional outfit in the box photo, you can tell Andersen's strangeness, his difference, which is to our benefit.

I was immediately drawn to one of his darkest tales, without a happy ending, but embracing a Jungian archetype, long before Jung himself was writing. 'The Shadow' was written in 1847 and was in Andersen's second collection of tales. It has a strange, modernist feel, perhaps having more in common with the fin de siécle poets and writers of later in the century, or even Oscar Wilde, who did borrow Andersen's story, just as Andersen himself had borrowed it for his own ends from the folklore of his country.

The introduction to the collection, by Dr Elias Bredsdorff, mentions that Andersen used to "listen to the old women in the spinning room of his native Odense", just as Burns received his oral story education from the women of his childhood. He wrote his tales as he would tell them, so he was again a traditionally creative type, never out of touch with his source of telling, however creative he was. Indeed, that is where he found the creativity itself. This plush book has about half of his output, which is not bad for 50p – and for a good, recent translation, by R.P. Keigwin. It was £15 for the cheapest copy of this book I could find on the internet.

'The Shadow' can be quickly told. It is a Faustian tragedy of the duality of repression, where the titular Shadow takes over the life of the 'real' person and the 'real' person dies. However, much can be drawn from the way he spins it, aside from obvious and easy parallels from his own life, of the kind which run the risk of being reductive of his art, which is considerable. I have a greater respect for Andersen from reading this tale a few times and I feel I want to go through it slowly, as if it were itself a boot sale of sights and insights that can be gained by slow, errant, picaresque deep reading. After this, I might well offer a continuation of the tale, or a version with – gasp! – a happy ending.

We are out of sorts and into duality from the beginning. A "learned man... had come straight from a cold country to a hot one". Like Faust, a bored student, opened to possibility, he has gone from one introverted world into the extreme opposite, or at least of the possibility of it, via his learning. Fairytales tend to warn against learning. I wrote a story myself called 'The Professor of Fables', which was a version of 'Tattercoats' from Joseph Jacobs' *More English Fairytales* (1894). This features in the postscript of my *Myth and Creative Writing* (2011). The 'learned' man is bound in his own hair and beard, weeping. This is a problem I don't have, owning little of either type of hair furniture myself.

Dualities are both the blessings of life and its curses. Creation itself is bound up in divisions, as the undifferentiated whole is divided into day and night, for example, in the Bible. These create good cycles, between which we can live and grow. I am living a good cyclic duality in the present writing, as I come to the end of the winter-autumn and move towards my beginning in the spring-summer. I am near the end of my self-imposed boot sale season's rhythm. I am in the pause before the beginning, the pause before the end. It is a time to reflect on beginnings and endings, on pasts and futures and hold them in balance.

Dualities that do not hold things in balance are extremes and Andersen's tale is one of extremism. We too live in an age of divisive extremism, of unsubtle sidedness, fed by the two-dimensional worlds of the internet. The creative mind can rock these balances and re-establish the gimbal that holds life's astrolabe together, if you don't mind me saying so. Andersen, so aware of this situation, this tendency, is able to inspire us with his failures and his deathly end is his beginning.

The Faust legend itself has its learned protagonist sell his soul to the devil and is the myth of our time in unsubtle, shocking form. This featured greatly in my next book *The Magic of Writing* (2018). Andersen's story is more of the time somehow because it is about the self in division, where the ambiguity, the paradox, is more subtle. For Jung, the Shadow is the key to the self and any improvement that it might achieve. The discovery of ambiguity, the learning of what is hidden, is a key part of the progress of the soul's maturation, and maturation is the common theme of many fairytales.

Fairytales invite us to trivialise them, until only children, or those with childlike imagination, the creatives, can easily find them meaningful. This is surely true of fairytale scholars. I remember hearing one of the most famous of these talking, and found myself remarking to a friend who taught on a course about fairytales, that this scholar did not even like his subject. This is all too common. Luckily, I knew the opposite person to this male one at the time. Dame Marina Warner is great on the tales, so much so that I always want to call her, as a complimentary joke, a Pantomime Dame. The tales invite extremes and are about balancing the extremes of immaturity with the possibility of maturity.

The cold-climated 'learned' man must wait in his new heat

till night for life to happen, out of the glare of the sun. His life has become its own metaphor, another aspect of myth and fairytale. Fairytale is often about its own doubts at reality and is usefully in discussion with itself.

The next thing is that in the shadowy but real world of night he sees a vision of a full life with flowers growing and music playing, which is hypnotic, like a perfect setting with no people, or a kind of Eden to create in. Then he sleeps but awakens and sees, as if still in a dream, a shining girl like a blessed being in paradise. He hides and the vision is gone.

He notices his shadow can reach the mysterious house opposite, even if he cannot, and he asks the shadow to go there. As he leaves his balcony, so his shadow does the same, but opposite. It is then we get the meta-textual mention of the well-known story of the "man without a shadow", and the man fears being a plagiarist, an "imitator". This is his third separation from the possibility of Edenic innocence. The hiding being the first, the second being the sending of his shadow.

He can still grow a new shadow at this point, but then his old shadow returns, quietly, as a man. This man is "distinguished" and "successful". At this point I began to think of the Peter O'Toole film *The Ruling Class*, where the Christ-like protagonist becomes Devil-like. Here, they begin the usual soul-bargaining, with a kind of inevitability even Andersen cannot escape. The shadow becomes 'the Shadow' and thus the stronger character. The Shadow says he found "poetry" across the street. He sees "everything". He knows both "nothing" and "everything". The Shadow tries to get the man to accompany him but his reunification fails. The theory and the practice fall apart. The tale has its own will, its own shadow, dependent but dark.

Then they do go away together, with roles reversed. But it does not go well. The Shadow gets the Princess. She thinks the man is the shadow of the Shadow. "My shadow has gone mad," says the Shadow. So complete reversal has happened and the man is doomed and, in the last line, dies.

Apart from anything else, at this point, I begin to think of the psychological truth of this archetypal situation, where life lived at a distance from the self takes over and the real becomes unreal, where mere reflection seems reality, where images are arranged and left in mirrors.

When you grow a great shadow, through the world's illness, for example a real pandemic or a shadow machine-driven through computers, the risk is that it becomes monstrous. But the monster is recognisably your own and can easily become you, unbalanced and overwhelming. Over-reaction is the order of the day. The great shadows of our recent time have been the isolation and real losses of the recent pandemic, which seem to be a collective monster we have created somehow, in our spoiled Eden, as it echoes the dark world of machines we have entered in shadow.

Practically, we might well take a long time to ungrow this huge shadow of the times. I feel unsure, unsafe and nervous myself, and boot sales were my normalcy, my crossing to the opposite balcony of light and "everything" and in the shadow part of the year, I am still going there, even as the sun is brightening, yet still chilled. My six months of writing, mirroring the six months of booting, are drawing to an end. The new season's boot sales will be starting and some may have started already, as I write.

The approach to poetry is difficult. We see the lighted muse and can only wonder what there is to see and we are led astray to see "everything" instead. Nic Jones' version of the song 'The Flandyke Shore' comes to mind, echoing the plot of Andersen's story: "I went unto my true love's chamber door / Where I never had been before / There I saw a light shining from her clothes... / Just as the morning sun when first arose." The luminous vision of transcendent life contrasts with the war and death themes of the whole, brief, enigmatic song, but the positive vision must be acknowledged even so, as must the fertility of the image, however misread or misused by the limits of learning.

Andersen's story is magical but there is no happy ending and no fairy, unless you count the image of the transcendent, luminous fertility opposite. His humility, or hiding from it via his shadow is not necessarily wrong, only human. The shadow must be independent but is always only a shadow too and has to be understood in this ambiguous light. The story does that, even though to see it as being for children can only itself be a shadow of its real meaning, which is the fear of what can be lost in growing to maturity. It there another story? Is there a part two, when we are all Shadows now, without shadows, in our pale, indoor, onscreen lives? Since the epic turned into tragedy we cannot do happy endings, except in a hidden or shadow way, but we must try, or give it up to the doomed celebrants of the apocalypse, who many writers have become. Being split in two by our either/or Western thinking, our 1 or 0 computers, we cannot think other than by division into extremes. Is there another myth, another balance?

A NEW SHADOW

Once upon a now, no-one had a shadow. Without innocence, you cannot learn from experience, only live it. The drive towards materialism was relentless and everyone lived in a bright blue spotlight and believed there was nothing else.

A woman called Sane was being driven mad by the light, which had now become the Light. A man called Mad offered her a lift, a ride into the ordinary forgotten world, the shadowed world, and Sane surprised herself by accepting. Mad said life was made by going there often, to the same place twice, but Sane said it would be fine as a novelty, but not real. So Sane and Mad split up. Neither realised that this split was not real and neither was the Light they seemed to have to obey.

Mrs Supernatural lived next door. She called on Mad and said, "You have joined the shadowless."

"What can I do to regain a shadow?" asked Mad.

"Go into the wilderness and seek your shadow. You will be tested and you must be so at home that you can accept the rest and every test and answer wholly to all. Go and seek the boot sale of shadows and wander as an errant among the bricolage and make something yourself out of it. Something which has a shadow. As above, so below, thence to balance. And if someone asks why you wander from cheerful day to take the downward melancholy way, say that the cheerful day has been stolen by the casual conspiracy of the greedy and turned into a blue spotlight. It has turned Sane mad. But it must turn Mad sane."

Mrs Supernatural left and Mad thought, this is all very helpful, but I don't know where to start. Then he went to the dance at the community centre, thinking that he would start the next day. But it was there, where people came to feel awkward, that the questions started, as they did in the story of The Shadow. For, as there, it is only the shadow that knows answers to the unanswerable.

Mad was dancing with a two-dimensional person, when he noticed that he was two-dimensional himself. But when the partner began asking him questions, the partner became three-dimensional. When he answered, remembering that he should be at home, he became three-dimensional in turn.

"Can you have infinite riches?"

"Yes, but at the cost of your soul, or your shadow, or your heart, or your Sane."

"Can you live forever?"

"No, as limits are life and you must step in the same place twice to know it at all. Infinity is an illusion of thinking in a dualistic, Western, divisive, profit-driven way. As above, so round goes the time below the limits of our questions."

"Can you own the whole world?"

"Sure thing, easily. We can do it now."

They found themselves laughing. By then, they both had shadows and were fully dimensional and could move out from the dance of non-shadows, who folded and collapsed around them. They took a step outside into the street and Mad showed the partner, the other, the shadowed shadow, the stars.

"Can we look up?" Mad asked the partner.

"Yes. We can turn away from the bright blue light and towards the light of the night sky. It is there we realise that the sky is light and only the Earth is dark."

"Where shall we go?" asked Mad.

"We will go up on to the hill, where there is another dance to be done and where you can see the light from the night sky, where all shadows come from."

Down the street and up the hill they went, both ignoring that they were fading into two dimensions, both nervous and both scared to speak of their nerves, despite their bravery in questions and in turning from the light. But something made them trudge on together, which was something and not nothing, however much they faded, or unshadowed.

On the hill, there was a midnight boot sale of shadows and they began to question and laugh again, as they wandered between the stalls and bought a small black dog who instinctively understood the good of shadows and was happy to wander and find good things.

When they had wandered enough, the temptations of fear came again, as they hesitated by the exit.

"Is there another dance to be done?" they asked the woman at the gate. As she turned to answer, she turned into Mrs Supernatural.

"Bless you, my children," she said.

Then people began to gather round them in a circle, as if for a dance. They were surrounded by good-seeming, shadowed people.

"I think I know all these people," said the partner.

"I think I know all these people," said Mad.

One of the people was Sane. One of them was shorter than the others and made them realise that the ring was one of protection. Although the shorter person offered little cover, or shadow, the others made up for them and the circle was stronger for having the shorter person in it. It was like a dance, or like a defence, or like a formation of birds in the sky. It was a whirl and a stillness, but it gave them back their shadow and they were able then to descend back into the darkness below the hill, as one, shadowed and unafraid, with their harvest of curative shadows.

On their way home they saw an awkward man, dressed

in 19th-century clothes, tall and strange, with a huge shadow, saying that he had lost his shadow. And yet he blessed them for their togetherness, even in his doomed "shred of life", as he put it, which he could see clearly, although he was drunk on his own outsiderdom and blind to his own vision and without knowing that his lack of shadow was an illusion that might be overcome.

Once upon a now, when no-one had a shadow, of course everyone really had a shadow all along and lights were only an isolating, human invention after all. Once upon a now, they at last went back to once upon a time.

Week 22: FOLK ART AND THE PEASANTS' REVOLT

WEDNESDAY 22ND SEPTEMBER 2021:
MARKS TEY.

Kipps. H.G. Wells.

The Longest Journey. E.M. Forster (Old Penguins). 2 for £1.

'John Ball and the Dragon' leaflet. £2.

Model violin. £1.50.

Blaming. Elizabeth Taylor. 50p.

Hohner melodica book. 50p.

New hat (as Weeks 9-10). £12.

Music holder from piano. £5.

New brush and dustpan. £4.

My last boot sale of the year was on a lovely sunny day and I began up in the smaller field at Marks Tey, where it tends to be more antiquey. The first stall holder I stopped at had manikins and skulls, all part of his art projects, and we immediately fell into conversation about making art and about skulls as a kind of *momento mori*, which reminded you to live as much as of death. Making the art was a key agreement in the conversation, already dealing with last things and somehow with beginnings. Boot sales are not ends in themselves, but portals that lead you somewhere and not just into the past.

The beginnings and ends of the boot sale year happen roughly at the time of the equinoxes, which are those half-yearly moments when the night and day are balanced, and seem to pause, towards lighter or darker things to come. Now that I check, 22nd September was actually the autumnal equinox in 2021 and it is getting near the spring equinox as I write. The new season may well have begun. For everything there is a season, as Ecclesiastes and Pete Seeger say and everything is on sale at the booty. Everything seemed to connect on that last one of the year for me, and at the end of my six months of balanced meditation. The harvest is still coming to fruition, in reading and thinking about the widening experience of a boot sale season as being the day in the day and the night of the year.

Books have predominated but not exclusively so. At the start of this book, I planned to pick a single item, in the main, to discuss from my log of purchases, but it seems to be that, by now in the year, in both half-years, I had better include everything in my harvesting embrace. Straight away it occurs to me that *Kipps* has a depiction of a male relative of Arthur Kipps and his bride, who buys things from auctions, of mixed blessing, and gives them to the couple in a kind of well-intended comedy of caring and generosity typical of the book. I cannot check the sources here, as the book has already gone to Bookshop Dave, but I enjoyed reading it and watched the old film, during the year, on 'Talking Pictures' on TV. Wells had the common touch before it was cool to do so, in this novel, as in *Mr Polly*.

The other Elizabeth Taylor, the great underrated novelist, is suitably under the radar these days. It was a rare thing to find a novel by her. This was her last one, in fact.

You mostly find second division books at boot sales, if you find any you want to buy. It is a salvage job for a bibliophile, but the forgotten or undiscovered classic can make a comeback and enrich you greatly, like a secret unavailable in your local Waterstones. Secondhand bookshops and independent bookshops are different, thank God. I am still reading and giving presents from the books I bought as well as supplying Bookshop Dave with a bit of B-list interest. My best books have been like real treasure houses to me. These are the Dave Occomore ballad history of Essex, *Curiosities of Essex* (Week 17), out of which I made two songs and *A Book of Magicians* (Week 3), which is still, as I browse bits of it, leading me to other authors and to a great regard for Roger Lancelyn Green.

Contemplating this last week, I thought I would read a bit more from Green's lovely book, so I chose a story called 'The Magician Who Wanted More' by another great tale collector/anthologist/creative, Andrew Lang (1844-1912). Magically this seemed to be a more positive tale than the one I had attempted last Week in answer to Andersen. Lang is exuberantly playing with his medium and having fun. This is again a man full of the creative world of fairytale. His collections, now very valuable, were mostly from other sources, but he also wrote his own stories. These are not so collectable as books. But this story, which I love, is from *Tales of a Fairy Court* and I excitedly find there is a damaged copy of this for sale cheap on the internet, which I intend to bid for tomorrow, as I write. If they are as good as this one, and as funny, this is another road opened up by a 50p purchase, which I shall go right down and get all his original stuff. I also remember an old PhD-time pal called Christopher Harris, who was working on Lang, and might look up his work.

The protagonist of the tale, Prigio, has "read all the books in the world", as his friend says, reminding me of Andersen and of a kind of boot sale attitude. Unlike Andersen's 'learned man', he wears his knowledge lightly and deals with what he comes across in the magical world with unpremeditated responses. He rescues his friend from despair and the world from a monster magician, who has captured all the lovely women, like a Patriarchy Bluebeard. Prigio casually releases them all from their extremity and overcomes the monster with some Champagne, newly invented. The story is effervescent and beautifully light in tone and a great fruitful beginning for me.

So many resonances here, as he looks at his watch, "a fairy time piece... which he had set... at *Present Day* and, lo, it read *Fairy Times*." This reminds me of my time-buying, in Week 2, and of my biannual structure of the current work. When I got to the bit about him wearing a "Wishing Cap", the coincidences appear like lost relatives and he carries a "pocket book" for notes (see Week 14). The fact that he wanders without trying, finding out all he needs to know, reminds me of the whole year. He is a kind of Fool as Mage humble wanderer, in his cap, with his notebook and his bibliophilia – and I am with him. I'll let you know if I get the book this tale comes from. (Latest news: I was the only bidder and I got it – a 'sleeper' is what we call a hidden bargain of value in books.)

Another humble Fool as Mage is the locally claimed John Ball, a trainee priest attached to St James' Church in East Hill, Colchester, who took up the peasants' cause and turned into a 'hedge priest'. I bought the John Ball leaflet having already written much about John Ball in a song and poem cycle, performed by my duo Face Furniture, with my friend Murray Griffin on double bass. Local vicar and author/activist Brian Bird published two books in his life. One was about skiffle music and the other was about John Ball: cue for a load of songs about skiffle and peasants.

The leaflet is called *John Ball and the Dragon*. There is a dragon in the Lang story and also a giant fly, which might be more of a good image for the parasitical exploitation of the poor that Ball was against. On the cover is an image made from a pen and ink drawing by Edward Burne-Jones of a Pre-Raphaelite Adam and Eve, with the text 'WHEN ADAM DELVED AND EVE SPAN / WHO WAS THEN THE GENTLEMAN'. This is the alleged text for John Ball's sermon and merely means that in the Garden of Eden there were no bosses exploiting anyone. The stylised picture comes from an illustration to the William Morris text *A Dream of John Ball* (1888). The leaflet was published in 1980 and originally cost 12p and is by Jack Putterill, "VICAR of THAXTED and Chairman of the Thaxted Branch of the National Union of Agricultural Workers." He was the son-in-law of Conrad Noel, the 'Red Vicar', a massively influential figure on folk music and his place and times. At the time of the leaflet, the church at Thaxted had a John Ball Chapel, but I am not sure they still do, or if they keep up their socialist legacy. Putterill was thinking about John Ball, as Brian Bird and others were in the 1980s, when exploitation seemed the order of the day again, which Putterill sees as a dragon to be "overthrown and slain", as he says, ending the leaflet. He was also the author of an autobiography and of the rare leaflet *Folk Dancing and Religion*, which sounds hilarious, though interesting.

It is the wide possibility of thinking about John Ball as a humble priest of equality and lost unity that makes me feel the openness of boot sales is there, like a kind of folk art, to be made by us all in a time of monstrous extremes. The news has turned from extreme pandemic to extreme war and this is all you hear, so I tune in less often than I did, even at the start of this season. *Richard II*, act 2:1 has its famous speech about England, but not often quoted are the lines about the island being "This fortress built by Nature itself / Against infection and the hand of war" (43-4). We have passed from the news of one to the news of the other, with no mention of the pandemic getting worse, as the numbers rise at present, as I write. Checking these lines again, I also like "this little world" in the next line. I think Shakespeare liked microcosm as an art, just as I think *The Tempest* is also about England. The boot sale is my humble, socialist, green little world of England and still my big world myth, as it was in Week 1.

When I began this venture, I also intended to write about things I did not buy, but I now realise this has not happened. Last week I saw something which attracted me, but I walked on. This was at Horsley Cross and was a handmade child's toy, a dog or monkey in a tin, which reminded me of the only childhood toy I still have, an old wooden dog, which was old I believe when I was given it. Thinking about art and my love for the commonality of the boot sale made me regret not buying the bit of folk art, as I feel yearnings towards what is sometimes called that. I do not mind such terms, even though they admit a prejudice. I like art that makes something out of what is around, done for sheer love and not out of a false sense of sophistication, or fashion. My own work is that down to earth I hope, and the boot sale reflects it, as my artist companion would have suggested.

With the John Ball leaflet, the Pre-Raphaelite drawing always looks too sophisticated to me, though they aspired to simplicity, but it is influenced by medieval art, which I also love.

Wearing my third hat from the hat seller (see Weeks 9-10) prompted a good chat with the man from London who said it was his last visit of the year. I told him that the similar one to the first one which I bought would be my best hat. Having read Lang's story, I now call it my wishing cap. "You will excuse my wearing my cap," says Prigio, as it gives him everything he wants. I have only worn these three caps all through the winter, from loads I love at home. An excellent stall and fine wishing hats.

The piano music holder is of the wooden kind that folds out from the lid of an upright piano. This I had seen before for a few weeks and thought of buying but could not find a justification. Knowing it was the last one of the year for me, made me decide that if it was under a tenner, I would have it. It was and I did. The chap said it was a very old one rescued from a broken piano. I later used it hung on the wall, with the John Ball leaflet, the John Piper book open at Fotheringhay church (Week 20) and a cut-out of a medieval painting of a band from the torn and dirty cover of the musical instrument book (Week 18). This art assemblage cheers its corner of the living room and again moves towards the folk art of my mind. I keep feeling I will make something myself but it might be a writing project.

Writing leads to writing and this year has been fantastically stimulating, with all its biannual reflection.

Even the new brush and pan, of the standing up kind and bright yellow, call to a sunny future in their folk plastic way, their cheap-shop bargain cheerfulness. Model violins are knick-knack-like people's art, but my niece will dig it, I hope, and the gift culture is again maintained. The Hohner melodica went out of fashion but bands in the 1990s began using them despite the fact they were no longer made. Naturally I bought a few at boot sales quite cheap. The book was also linked with harmonicas, and harnesses (Week 20), from the great German unintended folk company Hohner.

Buying at boot sales thus became an art form for me, an assemblage of openness to influence from everywhere. The whole world is spread out on an island of grass and the salvage of useful fittingness makes me a bigger person in the time when the world seems shrunken. Or, and even so, it is a nice walk among people with odd bargains and boons to be sought. I remember scavengers from my childhood, the men who collected rubbish seemingly without reason, walking round the streets, often with an old pram, as if salvage was their baby. I feel they did not have a reason, but an urge to assemble. Quite the opposite of the 'de-cluttering' culture of plenty. It might have come from the wartime shortages, or the collecting of metal for artillery shell-making. It seems instinctual and irrational in the main.

I think my friends, so into the world of the everyday, who would not have time to go to boot sales even if they could, partly envy me and partly see me as I saw those strange guys with prams. Artists understand, and my book-loving pals understand, and my ex's little dog knows well why the habit became my way of life in the latest emergencies. Not sure how much I will go, now that the new season has probably started as I write. Writing has led to writing and I need time to work on collections of poems and recordings of songs.

If I do go, it might well be with friends who have expressed an interest in going with me, as I have told them a little about the enthusiasms of this book, which sounds like fun. There is a nice pub called The Alma very near Marks Tey; a good place to go for lunch. I had hoped to go to sales outside my own area, but did not make it, as the weather and the times were against me. But this coming year I have some favourites in mind, up in Norfolk on my way to a holiday and one nearby where I will stay, for example. The small ones have community and the big ones diversity: the world is encompassed.

On a sunny, early autumn day, the harvest is the enjoyment and wide, ripe feel of the world, somehow without a thought for winter. Although I went home early, there was enough in my bag to carry, along with the music holder held like another bag in my hand. And enough to be thinking about. The new stand-up dustpan was the last thing I bought, so as to make only one journey back to the car. The day seemed full to itself, the year done and my log filled in. This has been mostly easy to read, although scribbled, with only one illegible purchase I think, though much not discussed and still lots to say. Some books, like Dave Occomore's and *A Book of Magicians* are still giving directly into my imagination and much fun. Many presents are remembered. I still have some local history for my pal Elaine's birthday, happening soon. The freedom of the market place and of the errant wanderer with his meagre purse of small change is a great grounder and leveller, and the lost village fair is recreated over and again. You can take the temperature of the times from its excess and discarded stuff and feel the community in the sellers' chat and relaxation, from the tense young dealer, eager for cash, to the wise old bird, who doesn't care much except to have a nice time and pay the fee for their stall's entry.

Although I know I have broken into song and even story at times, a short and meditative rhyme seems a good way to end, as one should always end on a song, in one way or another. In my case, an old-fashioned one. You need something that sings goodbye, as a ritual of ending, something aspiring at transcendence picked up along the way, in the big boot sale myth of life:

AT THE END OF THE BOOT SALE YEAR

At the end of the boot sale year
Hard to think this will soon disappear
There's no chill that you might feel in spring –
Then we don't mind; then it's all promising –
But for now in the sun we ignore all the rest

And enjoy the bright day and the boot sale harvest
The feeling of plenty is variously here
At the end of the boot sale year.

Ingram Content Group UK Ltd.
Milton Keynes UK
UKHW011842150523
421788UK00001B/1

9 781739 403805